HISTORIC DOUBTS
ON THE
LIFE AND REIGN
OF
KING RICHARD THE THIRD

Horace Walpole in 1754, engraved from the painting by
John Eccardt; Strawberry Hill in the background

HISTORIC DOUBTS
ON THE
LIFE AND REIGN
OF
KING RICHARD THE THIRD

INCLUDING THE
SUPPLEMENT, REPLY, SHORT
OBSERVATIONS AND POSTSCRIPT

HORACE WALPOLE

*With an introduction
and notes by*
P.W. HAMMOND

ALAN SUTTON
1987

ALAN SUTTON PUBLISHING
BRUNSWICK ROAD · GLOUCESTER

Copyright © in this edition 1987
Alan Sutton Publishing Limited
Copyright © in introduction and end notes
1987 P. W. Hammond

This edition first published 1987

British Cataloguing in Publication Data

Walpole, Horace
 Historic doubts on the life and reign of
 Richard III.
 1. Richard III, King of England
 I. Title
 942.04′6′0924   DA260
 ISBN 0–86299–299–0

Cover picture: David Garrick as Richard III *by
Hogarth. Walker Art Gallery, Liverpool.
Photograph: Bridgeman Art Library.*

Typesetting and origination by
Alan Sutton Publishing Limited.
Printed in Great Britain by
The Guernsey Press Company Limited
Guernsey, Channel Islands.

CONTENTS

INTRODUCTION

On 1 February 1768 the *Historic Doubts* of
Horace Walpole was published, in an edition of
1250 copies. Copies cost 5 shillings each, as
stated in the advertisement in the *London
Chronicle* of that day. These had all been sold by
the following day, and a reprint, a further 1000
copies, immediately put in hand, for publication by 12 February. Such an immediate
success caused both author and Dodsley, the
publisher, some surprise, but obvious pleasure,[1]
and in many ways the success has continued to
the present day, since the *Historic Doubts*
occupies an especial place in the historiography
of Richard III.

Walpole had been writing the book since the
winter of 1767,[2] and had been busily informing
all his friends of this, begging their help in the
research. He was writing to his friend Madame
du Deffand as early as April 1767 to tell her that

The abbreviation 'Yale' is used throughout for the Yale
edition of *Horace Walpole's Correspondence*, edited by W.S.
Lewis *et al*, 48 volumes, 1937–1983.

1.   *London Chronicle*, 1 February 1768, p. 169; letter
     to David Dalrymple, 2 February 1768, (Yale, vol.
     15, p. 119).
2.   See in the 'Short Notes on his Life', Walpole (Yale,
     vol. 13, p. 43), 1 February 1768: 'Published my
     Historic Doubts on Richard Third. I had begun it in
     the winter of 1767, continued it in the summer,
     and finished it on my return from Paris'.

he was 'at the moment working on the very interesting subject of the reign of our Richard III, who has been given a very bad character. I have discovered a most important record of his coronation, and very much doubt if he murdered his nephews'.[3] The record of the coronation referred to by Walpole, which he later called the 'Coronation Roll' was the cause of great excitement on his part, and he wrote about it to others of his correspondents.[4] It was not in fact a coronation roll, something which caused Walpole some problems later, but the Great Wardrobe Account covering the period of Richard's coronation (see below and the notes to the text), but demonstrates Walpole's desire to use original documents in his work. A letter from his antiquarian friend, Thomas Gray, in December 1767 answers some enquiries Walpole had made on documents in the important docket book of the Signet Office under Richard III.[5] Walpole printed two letters from

3. Yale, vol. 3, p. 287.
4. *Historic Doubts*, p. [65]; letters to David Dalrymple of 8 November 1767 and 17 January 1768, in the latter: 'I do not wonder you could not guess the discovery I have made. It is one of the most marvellous that ever was made. In short it is the original Coronation Roll of Richard III, by which it appears that very magnificent robes were ordered for Edward V, and that he did, or was to have walked at his uncle's coronation' (Yale, vol. 15, pp. 115, 117).
5. Letter from Gray, Yale, vol. 15, pp. 159–161; BL Harleian MS 433, now edited by Rosemary Horrox and P.W. Hammond (3 vols, Upminster and London, 1979–1982). The letters are on folio 2b (vol. 1, p. 2), and folio 340b (vol. 3, p. 259), *Historic Doubts*, pp. [39] and [118–119]. These are

this manuscript (Richard III to his mother, and to Thomas Lynom his Solicitor General), and a later letter asks Gray's help with a passage on Jane Shore, which seems to have given Walpole some trouble.[6] Notes made by Walpole in his copy of the 1759 *Catalogue* of the Harleian Manuscripts are still extant, from which it appears that he did look at the original himself.[7] Unfortunately in his use of them his citations of the source are inaccurate: compare Walpole's references to the source with the correct references above. His carelessness also extended to his extensive quotations from other sources such as the *Croyland Chronicle* and John Rous' *Historia Regum Angliae*, where words are sometimes misplaced or misquoted, and his quotation of More's work is from the corrupt version in Hall's Chronicle. This carelessness does not detract from his arguments or his use and appreciation of the value of the sources, an appreciation which not all of his contemporary critics seem to have achieved.

The publication of the *Historic Doubts* caused an immediate reaction. We have seen how quickly the first edition sold out, and reviews and comments immediately began to appear. The response was mixed. Walpole's friends were in general favourable in their response. His main antiquarian correspondent, William Cole, was the most enthusiastic, saying that 'It has pleased me beyond measure and thoroughly

articles numbers 6 and 2378 respectively in the 1759 catalogue.

6. Walpole to Gray, 6 March 1768, (Yale, vol. 14, pp. 180–181).
7. W.S. Lewis, *Rescuing Horace Walpole*, (Yale University Press, 1978), pp. 193, 194.

convinced me that if Richard was no saint, yet
he was not the sinner that he has been represented. It will be no easy task to refute the
arguments you have so masterly drawn up in his
favour'. Cole goes on to say that he was initially
rather prejudiced against Walpole's thesis.
Thomas Gray was slightly more reserved,
praising its clarity, and saying that he had read
it with attention and pleasure, but raising a few
objections.[8] Some of the public comments were
also quite favourable, eg. the reviewer in the
Monthly Review believed that 'greater justice
would now be done to Richard' and the reviewer
in the *London Chronicle* thoroughly discussed
Walpole's arguments, and ended up by agreeing
with him.[9] Other comment in the *London
Chronicle* was not so polite, in a series of articles
by 'Impartialis'. These articles are based on the
premiss that the author can find 'no contradiction' and 'no improbabilities' in the traditional
account of Richard, and are written in a very
hostile manner, almost as if exonerating
Richard from his 'crimes' was a personal affront
to the author.[10] All of these reviews, and a

8.   10 February 1768, (Yale, vol. 1, p. 128); Cole
     repeats his previous comments in a letter of 9 July
     1772, (Yale, vol. 1, p. 268); letter from Gray, 14
     February 1768, (Yale, vol. 14, pp. 161–165).
9.   That in the *Monthly Review*, (vol. 38 (February),
     pp. 114–125), was by Andrew Kippis, who later
     violently disagreed with Walpole's arguments, see
     letter to Walpole from William Cole, 1 March
     1780 (Yale, vol. 2, pp. 196–197); the first part at
     least of the *London Chronicle* review, (in two parts,
     pp. 129–130 of 6–9 February issue, and pp.
     137–138 of 9–11 February), must have been
     written in a great hurry unless prepublication
     copies were sent out.

longer production signed 'FWG'[11] tended to criticise Walpole's arguments by taking his words or quotations and denying that they could bear his meaning, they did not in general criticise him by bringing other documents to bear on the arguments. This was done in one early review, that by William Guthrie in the *Critical Review*.[12] He criticises Walpole severely, complaining of his lack of research, and referring to documents himself to refute him, eg Tyrell's patent as one of the commissioners for the office of Constable from Rymer's *Foedera*, a point Walpole meets in his own answers, (see below). Walpole had previously been at odds politically with Guthrie, but the chief cause of Guthrie's spleen seems to have been that Walpole did not refer to his *History of England* in the *Historic Doubts*. This annoyance was to some extent justified since Guthrie, although tradi-

10. *London Chronicle*, 6 issues between that for 10–12 March 1768 and 28–31 May 1768, together with a letter from 'Sceptic' supporting Walpole in the 17–19 March issue, a letter from 'Impartialis' in 29–31 March criticising 'Sceptic', and one from an anonymous supporter of 'Impartialis' in that of 23–26 April.

11. F.W. Guidickens a lawyer 'of the Middle Temple', in *An Answer to Mr Horace Walpole's Late Work entitled Historic Doubts*, 1768. FWG is not convinced by Walpole, he reasonably comments indeed that 'It is remarkable that Mr Walpole picks and chuses from Historians only as it may answer his purpose, though ever so weakly; and then he puts what sense or interpretations he pleases upon his authorities', p. 45, note a.

12. William Guthrie, *Critical Review*, vol. 25, (February), pp. 116–126. Walpole thought that FWG was Guthrie too (a letter to George Montague, 12 March 1768, Yale, vol. 10, pp. 234).

tional in tone concerning the death of the Princes, had queried Richard's responsibility for the death of Henry VI, nor did he wholly disbelieve that Perkin Warbeck could have been the Duke of York, one of Walpole's chief arguments. Walpole admitted that he had never seen Guthrie's work. [13]

Walpole could, and did, dismiss these critics with some scorn, he described 'Impartialis' as a 'hackney historian' whom he refused to enquire after. [14] He could not do as much for his three most serious critics, David Hume the historian, the Reverend Doctor Jeremiah Milles, Dean of Exeter and President of the Society of Antiquaries, of which Walpole was a member, and the Reverend Mr Robert Masters. Walpole had been nervous of Hume's response, he had indeed probably consulted him about the work in the course of 1767. [15] Hume had apparently shown Walpole some manuscript notes on the controversy in that same year, but it was not until they were published in 1769 in the *Memoires litteraires* at the end of an anonymous review in French, (to which they were appended as 16 notes also in French), that Walpole was really roused. The review was in fact by Edward Gibbon, but Walpole thought that it was by the editor Jean-Jacques Deyverdun. [16] Hume had

13. William Guthrie, *History of England*, (1747), vol. 2, pp. 719–720, 809–831, particularly 809 and 831; Walpole to Gray, 8 March 1778, (Yale, vol. 14, p. 181, and see pp. 130–31 below).
14. Letter to Cole, 6 June 1768, (Yale, vol. 1, p. 144).
15. For example, see letters to William Cole, 16 April 1768, (Yale, vol. 1, pp. 133–134) and to Thomas Gray, 26 February 1768, (Yale, vol. 14, p. 176).
16. The review was in *Memoires litteraires de la Grande*

begged Walpole to give Deyverdun a copy of *Lord Herbert's Life* (published by Walpole at his press at Strawberry Hill) to help Deyverdun with this second volume of the *Memoires*. When the critical review of *Historic Doubts* appeared in this Walpole regarded this as treachery. The review proper of *Historic Doubts* was quite mild, and not too unfavourable to Walpole, but finally concluded that Hume's traditional view was probably correct. The next damaging piece of work to appear, (it was not really a review), was that by Milles. Milles read a paper at a meeting of the Antiquaries in March 1770, entitled 'Observations on the Wardrobe Account for the year 1483'.[17] This was a trenchantly worded discussion of Walpole's 'Coronation Roll' in which Milles pointed out its true nature, and that robes described there for 'Edward V' were ordered while he was still King, and certainly did not show that he was intended to walk in his uncle's coronation procession, as Walpole had argued. Masters also questioned Walpole's identification of James Tyrell as the Master of the Horse at the coronation. His comments went a little further than his evidence allowed, but were on the whole a damaging criticism of some of Walpole's main arguments. Following fairly quickly after this was another paper given to the Antiquaries in January 1771 by Robert Masters,

Bretagne, vol. 2, pp. 1–35. For Walpole's belief on authorship see letter to Mason 18 February 1776, (Yale, vol. 28, p. 246); letter from Hume, 11 November 1768, (Yale, vol. 41, pp. 166–167); see also Walpole's 'Short Notes', under 1769, (Yale, vol. 13, p. 44).

17.   Published in *Archaeologia*, by the Society of Antiquaries, vol. 1 (1770), pp. 361–383.

'Some Remarks on Mr Walpole's Historic Doubts'.[18] This was designed in many ways as a supplement to Milles' article, but made some new comments of his own, notably that Eleanor Butler was not descended from the Stafford Dukes of Buckingham as Walpole had said. He was also very much more ascerbic in his tone. This Walpole at least attributed to his own refusal to respond to Masters' flattery.[19]

Walpole in his correspondence was dismissive of these attacks, preferring to ridicule them, and belittle their comments. He said for example that he was in no hurry to see an offprint of Masters' article.[20] In reality, they seem to have stung him considerably, particularly the 'tacks of Milles and Masters, who as fellow members of the Society of Antiquaries he expected to be more circumspect in their criticisms. Collectively, they all stung him sufficiently to cause him to write three replies, his 'Supplement', which answered his immediate critics, particularly Hume's points, his 'Reply to the Observations of the Reverend Doctor Milles', and his 'Short Observations on the Remarks of the Reverend Mr Masters'. The first two were composed on 10 May and 6 August 1769, the dates appended to the 'Supplement', and 18 August 1770, the date at the end of the 'Reply'. The 'Short Observations' is not dated but Walpole refers to it in a letter to William Cole

18. Published in *Archaeologia*, vol. 2 (1771), pp. 198–215.
19. Letter to Mason, 18 February 1776, (Yale, vol. 28, p. 247).
20. For example in his letters to Cole, 11 June 1771 and 8 January 1773, (Yale, vol. 1, pp. 219, 294).

in April 1773.[21] It seems probable that Walpole drafted the first two replies in preparation for publication, (at his Strawberry Hill press) in his projected *Complete Works* of 1770. This was abandoned, possibly as late as 1774, after Volume One and part of Volume Two had been printed. Volume Two had reached *Historic Doubts*, the 'Supplement', the 'Reply' and 'Short Observations'. The 'Reply' had been printed separately as a pamphlet by 1771.[22] Walpole obviously took considerable trouble over the 'Supplement' at least. What is apparently a first version, presumably for the 1770 *Complete Works* was published in 1860.[23] It is identical to that finally published in the *Complete Works* of 1798 except for one passage at the end.[24] This consists of comments on observations of a 'learned dignitary of the Church' and appears to be the brief first draft of what later became 'A Reply'. As a case, it is considerably weaker than the 'Reply', but relies on much the same arguments.

These replies of Walpole to his critics are on the whole only moderately effective, certainly not as effective as he himself believed. His friends, particularly William Cole, assured

21. Letter to Cole, 27 April 1773, (Yale, vol. 1, p. 308). Walpole in his 'Short notes' dates it to the beginning of 1774 or the end of 1773, (Yale, vol. 13, p. 49).
22. See A.T. Hazen, *A Bibliography of the Strawberry Hill Press* (London, 1942), pp. 89, 95. See also A.T. Hazen, *A Bibliography of Horace Walpole*, (London, 1948), p. 73.
23. 'Supplement to the Historic Doubts', edited by E.C. Hawtry in *Miscellanies of the Philobiblon Society*, vol. 6, (1860–61).
24. *Miscellanies*, pp. 96–100.

Walpole that, eg Masters' piece was 'a heap of rubbish . . . Trifles of objections which you will never give yourself the trouble to think of' and Walpole wrote later to Cole, after he had seen Masters' article, that he believed that Masters' arguments, particularly those on Eleanor Butler, were very weak and confused. He declared that 'If he [Masters] had not taken such pains to declare it was written against my *Doubts*, I should have thought it was a defence of them'. Such an attitude, which Walpole adopted in his printed 'Short Observations', must have infuriated Masters, to whom no doubt it would be communicated. To Lord Dacre, Walpole commented that he had 'a quantity of replies to Dr Milles and the rest of the childish or rather womanish replies to my book'. He wrote to Cole that he was not to mention the replies he had made to Masters and Milles, (and which he had shown to Cole), since he wished to surprise them should they bring out some new evidence which they supposed supported their case. [25]

It is obvious from the remarks above, that the dispute had become personal, and was no longer, if it ever had been, merely an argument over a disputed interpretation of history. To some extent this was probably Walpole's own

25. Letter from William Cole, 6 January 1773, (Yale, vol. 1, p. 290); to Cole, 7 April 1773, (Yale, vol. 1, p. 304); letter to Lord Dacre, 4 March 1777, (Yale, vol. 41, p. 356); letter to Cole, 27 April 1773, (Yale, vol. 1 p. 308). In a later letter Cole expressed a wish that Walpole would publish his 'tract' against Dean Milles, obviously because he believed it would be to Milles' discredit, 30 January 1776, (Yale vol. 2 p. 6).

fault, since in his Introduction to the *Historic Doubts* he was less than polite about historians who drew a picture of Richard III as a 'character formed by prejudice and invention'. Walpole's detached and ironic attitude towards his critics cannot have helped. He obviously did not always rate their understanding of their subject very highly. In the Introduction again he begins 'So incompetent has the generality of historians been for the province they have undertaken . . .'. He even describes Hume as 'very thick' in conversation, and his conduct over the French review (see above) as 'paltry'.[26] To add to this attitude of Walpole's was the fact that historians may not have liked, or wished to dissociate themselves from, the use he made of material which they had communicated to him. This was apparently particularly the case with the antiquary Thomas Astle, with whom Walpole had been on very good terms up to about April 1768. Astle had been one of those who had drawn Walpole's attention to books and documents, in this case particularly to the 'Coronation Roll', apparently by that designation. Once the mistake became known Astle probably did not wish to emphasise his part in it. After a long break in their correspondence he apparently sent Walpole a copy of the attainder of the Duke of Clarence, from the *Rolls of Parliament*, (which he was then editing), querying if it might not be a forgery by Richard of Gloucester to conceal his murder of Clarence. This absurd idea Walpole treated with glee in

26.   Letter to John Pinkerton, 22 June 1785, (Yale, vol. 16, p. 266, note 17); 'Short Notes', 24 April 1769, (Yale, vol. 13 p. 45).

his correspondence and with solemnity in his reply to Astle.[27]

Walpole refused to publish the replies he had written and of which he was so proud, on the grounds that he would have no controversy while he lived. As he put it to William Mason 'my answers [to his critics] shall sometime or other appear when I only shall be blamed and my antagonists will be dead and not hurt by them'.[28] Since he did not publish indeed, this position was obviously the one which he did in fact adopt, but one cannot help feeling that it also deprived his critics of any chance of replying, so that Walpole had the last word. This seems to have been his attitude towards his *Memoirs*, also not published until after his death. Walpole's critics cannot have been unaware of his views, both of them and of their ideas, since he took no great trouble to conceal either, and his one public gesture, resignation from the Society of Antiquaries, would in any case have made his attitude fairly clear. He resigned in July 1772, soon after he had heard from William Cole that Masters' attack on him was to be published in *Archaeologia*. As he said 'as there seems to be a willingness to carp at me, and as

27. For Astles part in the use of the 'Roll', *Historic Doubts* p. [65]; letters to and from Astle of 3 August 1767, 26 January 1768, 22 April 1768 and 19 December 1775, (Yale, vol. 41, pp. 95, 121–122, 144, 322–324); letter to Cole describing Astle's letter, 26 January 1776, (Yale, vol. 2, pp. 2–3); to Mason, 21 December 1775, (Yale, vol. 28, pp. 238–239).
28. Letter to Cole, 4 July 1780, (Yale, vol. 2 p. 229); to Mason, 18 February 1776, (Yale, vol. 28, p. 246).

gnats may on a sudden provoke one to give a slap I choose to be at liberty to say what I think of the learned Society, and have therefore taken leave of them'. He gave as his public reason for resignation the ridicule cast on the Society in a play satirising a talk on Dick Whittington and his cat given at the Society in 1771. That this was an excuse he admits in his 'Short Notes', he obviously felt that they had treated him without the respect which was his due. His resignation seems to have been received with regret by at least some of the other Fellows.[29]

Following the major criticisms discussed above, the controversy died down somewhat but did not cease. Walpole does not, (immediately at least) seem to have sown the seeds of doubt as he wished, not at least in an anonymous author whose long criticism appeared six years before Walpole died. This summed up his views as 'mere sophisticated casuistry'.[30] Criticism has not ceased yet. In 1858, James Gairdner considered it worth while to spend some time discussing and rejecting Walpole's views on Perkin Warbeck, and in 1898 Gairdner again considered and rejected Walpole's arguments. Interestingly enough, he thought it worth again pointing out Walpole's mistake over 'Edward V' walking in Richard III's coronation procession. Alison Hanham in 1975 quoted approvingly Walpole's view of Thomas More as an historian,

29. 'Short Notes', (Yale, vol. 13, p. 47); letter from Cole, 9 July 1772, (Yale, vol. 1, p. 268); to Cole, 28 July 1772, (Yale, vol. 2, p. 270); regret of some Fellows, from Cole, 7 March 1781, (Yale, vol. 2, p. 264).
30. Anon, *Free and Candid Remarks on Mr Walpole's Historic Doubts* (London, 1791), p. 64.

although she was unable to approve of his thesis as a whole.[31] Walpole never ceased to collect more information and evidence concerning his doubts, he borrowed the English version of the Rous Roll from the Duke of Manchester, the then owner, and as well as asking Thomas Astle if he could find someone to help him transcribe it, he decided to have some of the drawings engraved for use in a future edition of the *Historic Doubts*.[32] He enquired about Perkin Warbeck from various correspondents, from one of them (David Dalrymple), only the day after *Historic Doubts* was published. As late as 1791 he was writing to Samuel Lysons to ask him to verify an entry in the Harleian Manuscript 433 in the British Museum. This he said would confirm what he had said in *Historic Doubts* about Richard's treatment of his nieces and nephews.[33]

The *Historic Doubts* was the last of Walpole's

31.　James Gairdner, *Memorials of King Henry the Seventh* (London, 1858), pp. xxxiv, xxv, xxvi; *History of the Life and reign of Richard the Third* (London, 1898), particularly p. 101; Alison Hanham, *Richard III and his early historians 1483–1535* (London, 1975), pp. 155, 191, 197.

32.　Letter to Thomas Astle, 22 April 1768, (Yale, vol. 41, p. 144); engravings from Rous Roll, letter to Cole, 16 April 1768, (Yale, vol. 1, pp. 133, 134). The engravings were published in the *Complete Works* of 1798, (vol. 2).

33.　Letter to Dalrymple, 2 February 1768 and from Dalrymple, 9 February 1768, (Yale, vol. 15, pp. 118–119, 120–121); see also letters to and from Thomas Gray, 18 February 1768, 25 February 1768, 26 February 1768, (Yale, vol. 14, pp. 168, 173–174, 175–176); letter to Lysons, 13 September 1792, (Yale, vol. 15, pp. 221–222).

major works to be published, and his most sustained piece of historical argument. He had a love of history, and a considerable influence in the world of the antiquaries through his published work, and through his extensive corespondence. In the latter he put his knowledge and time at the disposal of his friends and acquaintances. He wrote to old and young on the same terms, regarding them all as being engaged in a common search for truth as he was himself. It has been said that his historical writing was the most important part of his work, that in *Historic Doubts* in particular Walpole's passion for the truth was most evident, and that into it he put a considerable amount of thought.[34] He certainly put into it a considerable amount of work. He used a great many printed sources, the main one being *The History of King Richard the Third* by George Buck, but he also used the *Croyland Chronicle* (written in 1486) and Rous' *Historia* as mentioned above. Both of these latter were written by contemporaries of Richard III. The Tudor chroniclers, More, Hall and Fabyan he used more cautiously. As we have seen, Walpole certainly regarded *Historic Doubts* as much more important than the rather careless words, 'The attempt [to elucidate the mystery of Richard III] was a mere matter of curiosity and speculation', in the Introduction would indicate.[35]

34. Paul Yvon, *La Vie d'un Dilettante: Horace Walpole (1717–1797)* (Paris, 1924), Book 4, chap. 6, pp. 646–674, particularly pp. 646, 661; see also Yale, vol. 15, pp. xxxi and xxxiv.
35. Introduction, p. [xv]. Walpole habitually used similar words in his introductions, or in comments to friends to disarm criticism.

The book holds an important place in the historiography of Richard III, as the first widely circulated, (and certainly the most readable), attempt to point out the flaws in the traditional account of Richard III as derived from the Tudor historians, and to use extensively 15th century documents to do so. For this alone it deserves to be read, but the sprightly style, (and Walpole always believed that there was no reason why 'antiquarian' writings should be unreadable), and interesting subject matter also make it very enjoyable to read.

One last thing remains to be said. In 1800 there was published a French translation of the *Historic Doubts*. The translator was Louis XVI, and in his Introduction the Editor said that Louis had worked on the book while he was imprisoned in the Tuileries. There is now very little doubt that the translation was in fact by Louis XVI (it had been claimed by his brother Louis XVIII), and it fits rather poignantly with Walpole's 'Postscript to Historic Doubts Written in February 1793'.[36] This, written just after the execution of Louis XVI was Walpole's final word on the subject. In it he says that his belief that no one could have committed the crimes

36. See Lewis, *Rescuing Horace Walpole*, p. 197 for a reproduction of the first page of the manuscript of the translation. For the claim by Louis XVIII, Colin Duckworth, 'Louis XVI and English History: a French reaction to Walpole, Hume and Gibbon on Richard III', *Studies in Voltaire and the 18th Century*, vol. 176, pp. 385–401, particularly pp. 385–388. That Louis XVI owned Historic Doubts was shown by G. Lambon, 'Louis XVI Angliciste', *Etudes Anglaises*, vol. 22, 1967, p. 123.

attributed to Richard III had been, if not destroyed, severely shaken. After the recent events in France he could certainly believe now (he carefully did not say he did), that Richard could have committed such crimes. A sad ending to his interest in the subject.

BIBLIOGRAPHIC NOTE

The first edition of the *Historic Doubts* was published, as already stated, on 1 February 1768. The second edition was published on 12 February 1768, and was almost identical to the first edition, except for the correction of the errata. The present version is entirely reset, using the text of the second edition. The versions in the *Complete Works* of 1770 and 1798 appear to have been taken from the first edition, as was a new edition published in London in 1822. This was reset and repaginated, but the errata slip was not adapted to the new pagination. A condensed version was published in London in 1965.[37] The 'Supplement', the 'Reply' and the 'Short Observations' were published in the Complete Works of 1798, volume 2, pp. 185–220, 221*–244* and 245*–251* respectively. The 'Postscript' appeared in volume 2 pp. 251*–252*. (These page numbers are asterisked in the original edition.)

Editorial notes on p. 266 ff. are indicated by asterisks in this edition of the text.

37. For more bibliographic details see Hazen, *A Bibliography of Horace Walpole*, p. 72. The 1965 edition was edited by P.M. Kendall, together with More's *History*, and published by the Folio Society.

HISTORIC DOUBTS
ON THE
LIFE AND REIGN
OF
KING RICHARD THE THIRD

L'Histoire n'est fondée que sur le temoignage des Auteurs qui nous l'ont transmise. Il importe donc extremement, pour la sçavois, de bien connoitre quels etoient ces Auteurs. Rien n'est à negliger en ce point; le tems où ils ont vecû, leur nassance, leur patrie, la part qu'ils ont eue aux affaires, les moyens par lesquels ils ont été instruits, et l'intérêt qu'ils y pouvoient prendre, sont des circonstances essentielles qu'il n'est pas permis d'ignorer: delà depend le plus ou le moins d'autorité qu'ils doivent avoir: et sans cette conoissance, on courra risque très souvent de prendre pour guide un Historien de mauvaise foi, ou du moins, mal informé.

Hist. de l'Acad. des Inscript. Vol. X.

PREFACE

So incompetent has the generality of historians been for the province they have undertaken, that it is almost a question, whether, if the dead of past ages could revive, they would be able to reconnoitre the events of their own times, as transmitted to us by ignorance and misrepresentation. All very ancient history, except that of the illuminated Jews, is a perfect fable. It was written by priests, or collected from their reports; and calculated solely to raise lofty ideas of the origin of each nation. Gods and demi-gods were the principal actors; and truth is seldom to be expected where the personages are supernatural. The Greek historians have no advantage over the Peruvian, but in the beauty of their language, or from that language being more familiar to us. Mango Capac, the son of the sun, is as authentic a founder of a royal race, as the progenitor of the Heraclidæ. What truth indeed could be expected, when even the identity of person is uncertain? The actions of one were ascribed to many, and of many to one. It is not known whether there was a single Hercules or twenty.

As nations grew polished, History became better authenticated. Greece itself learned to speak a little truth. Rome, at the hour of its fall, had the consolation of seeing the crimes of its usurpers published. The vanquished inflicted eternal wounds on their conquerors – but who

3

knows, if Pompey had succeeded, whether Julius Cæsar would not have been decorated as a martyr to publick liberty? At some periods the suffering criminal captivates all hearts; at others, the triumphant tyrant. Augustus, drenched in the blood of his fellow-citizens, and Charles Stuart, falling in his own blood, are held up to admiration. Truth is left out of the discussion; and odes and anniversary sermons give the law to history and credulity.

But if the crimes of Rome are authenticated, the case is not the same with its virtues. An able critic has shown that nothing is more problematic than the history of the three or four first ages of that city. As the confusions of the state increased, so do the confusions in its story. The empire had masters, whose names are only known from medals. It is uncertain of what princes several empresses were the wives. If the jealousy of two antiquaries intervenes, the point becomes inexplicable. Oriuna, on the medals of Carausius, used to pass for the moon: of late years it is become a doubt whether she was not his consort. It is of little importance whether she was moon or empress: but how little must we know of those times, when those land-marks to certainty, royal names, do not serve even that purpose! In the cabinet of the king of France are several coins of sovereigns, whose country cannot now be guessed at.

The want of records, of letters, of printing, of critics; wars, revolutions, factions, and other causes, occasioned these defects in ancient history. Chronology and astronomy are forced to tinker up and reconcile, as well as they can, those uncertainties. This satisfies the learned — but what should we think of the reign of George

4

the Second, to be calculated two thousand years hence by eclipses, lest the conquest of Canada should be ascribed to James the First?

At the very moment that the Roman empire was resettled, nay, when a new metropolis was erected, in an age of science and arts, while letters still held up their heads in Greece; consequently, when the great outlines of truth, I mean events, might be expected to be established; at that very period a new deluge of error burst upon the world. Christian monks and saints laid truth waste; and a mock sun rose at Rome, when the Roman sun sunk at Constantinople. Virtues and vices were rated by the standard of bigotry; and the militia of the church became the only historians. The best princes were represented as monsters; the worst, at least the most useless, were deified, according as they depressed or exalted turbulent and enthusiastic prelates and friars. Nay, these men were so destitute of temper and common sense, that they dared to suppose that common sense would never revisit the earth: and accordingly wrote with so little judgment, and committed such palpable forgeries, that if we cannot discover what really happened in those ages, we can at least be very sure what did not. How many general persecutions does the church record, of which there is not the smallest trace? What donations and charters were forged, for which those holy persons would lose their ears, if they were in this age to present them in the most common court of judicature? Yet how long were these impostors the only persons who attempted to write history!

But let us lay aside their interested lies, and consider how far they were qualified in other respects to transmit faithful memorials to posterity. In the ages I speak of, the barbarous monkish ages, the shadow of learning that existed was confined to the clergy: they generally wrote in Latin, or in verse, and their compositions in both were truly barbarous. The difficulties of rhime, and the want of correspondent terms in Latin, were no small impediments to the severe march of truth. But there were worse obstacles to encounter. Europe was in a continual state of warfare. Little princes and great lords were constantly skirmishing and scrambling for trifling additions of territory, or wasting each others borders. Geography was very imperfect; no police existed; roads, such as they were, were dangerous; and posts were not established. Events were only known by rumour, from pilgrims, or by letters carried by couriers to the parties interested: the public did not enjoy even those fallible vehicles of intelligence, newspapers. In this situation did monks, at twenty, fifty, an hundred, nay, a thousand miles distance (and under the circumstances I have mentioned even twenty miles were considerable) undertake to write history – and they wrote it accordingly.

If we take a survey of our own history, and examine it with any attention, what an unsatisfactory picture does it present to us! How dry, how superficial, how void of information! How little is recorded besides battles, plagues, and religious foundations! That this should be the case, before the Conquest, is not surprizing. Our empire was but forming itself, or re-collecting its divided members into one mass, which, from the desertion of the Romans, had split into petty kingdoms. The invasions of nations as barbarous as ourselves, interfered with every plan of policy and order that might have been formed to settle the emerging state; and swarms of foreign monks were turned loose upon us with their new faith and mysteries, to bewilder and confound the plain good sense of our ancestors. It was too much to have Danes, Saxons, and Popes to combat at once!

Our language suffered as much as our government; and not having acquired much from our Roman masters, was miserably disfigured by the subsequent invaders. The unconquered parts of the island retained some purity and some precision. The Welsh and Erse tongues wanted not harmony: but never did exist a more barbarous jargon than the dialect, still venerated by antiquaries, and called *Saxon*. It was so uncouth, so inflexible to all composition, that the monks, retaining the idiom, were reduced to write in what they took or meant for Latin.

The Norman tyranny succeeded, and gave this Babel of savage sounds a wrench towards their own language. Such a mixture necessarily required ages to bring it to some standard: and, consequently, whatever compositions were formed during its progress, were sure of growing obsolete. However, the authors of those days were not likely to make these obvious reflections; and indeed seem to have aimed at no one perfection. From the Conquest to the reign of Henry the Eighth it is difficult to discover any one beauty in our writers, but their simplicity. They told their tale, like story-tellers; that is, they related without art or ornament; and they related whatever they heard. No councils of princes, no motives of conduct, no remoter springs of action, did they investigate or learn.

We have even little light into the characters of the actors. A king, or an archbishop of Canterbury are the only persons with whom we are made much acquainted. The barons are all represented as brave patriots; but we have not the satisfaction of knowing which of them were really so; nor whether they were not all turbulent and ambitious. The probability is, that both kings and nobles wished to encroach on each other: and if any sparks of liberty were struck out, in all likelihood it was contrary to the intention of either the flint or the steel.

Hence has it been thought necessary to give a new dress to English history. Recourse has been had to records, and they are far from corroborating the testimonies of our historians. Want of authentic materials has obliged our later writers to leave the mass pretty much as they found it. Perhaps all the requisite attention that might have been bestowed, has not been bestowed. It demands great industry and patience to wade into such abstruse stores as records and charters: and they being jejune and narrow in themselves, very acute criticism is necessary to strike light from their assistance. If they solemnly contradict historians in material facts, we may lose our history; but it is impossible to adhere to our historians. Partiality man cannot intirely divest himself of; it is so natural, that the bent of a writer to one side or the other of a question is almost always discoverable. But there is a wide difference between favouring and lying – and yet I doubt whether the whole stream of our historians, misled by their originals, have not falsified one reign in our annals in the grossest manner. The moderns are only guilty of taking on trust what they ought to have examined more scrupulously, as the authors whom they copied were all ranked on one side in a flagrant season of party. But no excuse can be made for the original authors, who, I doubt, have violated all rules of truth.

The confusions, which attended the civil war between the houses of York and Lancaster, threw an obscurity over that part of our annals, which it is almost impossible to dispel. We have scarce any authentic monuments of the reign of Edward the Fourth; and ought to read his history with much distrust, from the boundless partiality of the succeeding writers to the opposite cause. That diffidence should increase as we proceed to the reign of his brother.

It occurred to me some years ago, that the picture of Richard the Third, as drawn by historians, was a character formed by prejudice and invention. I did not take Shakespeare's tragedy for a genuine representation, but I did take the story of that reign for a tragedy of imagination. Many of the crimes imputed to Richard seemed improbable; and, what was stronger, contrary to his interest. A few incidental circumstances corroborated my opinion; an original and important instrument was pointed out to me last winter, which gave rise to the following sheets; and as it was easy to perceive, under all the glare of encomiums which historians have heaped on the wisdom of Henry the Seventh, that he was a mean and unfeeling tyrant, I suspected that they had blackened his rival, till Henry, by the contrast, should appear in a kind of amiable light. The more I examined their story, the more I was confirmed in my opinion:– and with regard to Henry, one consequence I could not help drawing; that we have either no authentic memorials of Richard's crimes, or, at most, no account of them but from Lancastrian historians; whereas the vices and injustice of Henry are, though palliated, avowed by the concurrent testimony of his panegyrists. Suspicions and calumny were fastened on Richard as so many assassinations. The murders committed by Henry were indeed executions — and executions pass for prudence with prudent historians; for when a successful king is chief justice, historians become a voluntary jury.

If I do not flatter myself, I have unravelled a considerable part of that dark period. Whether satisfactorily or not, my readers must decide. Nor is it of any importance whether I have or not. The attempt was mere matter of curiosity and speculation. If any man, as idle as myself, should take the trouble to review and canvass my arguments, I am ready to yield so indifferent a point to better reasons. Should declamation alone be used to contradict me, I shall not think I am less in the right.

Nov. 28th, 1767.

HISTORIC DOUBTS ON THE
LIFE AND REIGN OF
KING RICHARD THE THIRD

There is a kind of litterary superstition, which
men are apt to contract from habit, and which
makes them look on any attempt towards
shaking their belief in any established characters, no matter whether good or bad, as a sort of
prophanation. They are determined to adhere to
their first impressions, and are equally offended
at any innovation, whether the person, whose
character is to be raised or depressed, were
patriot or tyrant, saint or sinner. No indulgence
is granted to those who would ascertain the
truth. The more the testimonies on either side
have been multiplied, the stronger is the
conviction; though it generally happens that the
original evidence is wonderous slender, and that
the number of writers have but copied one
another; or, what is worse, have only added to
the original, without any new authority.
Attachment so groundless is not to be regarded;
and in mere matters of curiosity, it were
ridiculous to pay any deference to it. If time
brings new materials to light, if facts and dates
confute historians, what does it signify that we
have been for two or three hundred years under
an error? Does antiquity consecrate darkness?
Does a lie become venerable from its age?

Historic justice is due to all characters. Who
would not vindicate Henry the Eighth or

Charles the Second, if found to be falsely traduced? Why then not Richard the Third? Of what importance is it to any man living whether or not he was as bad as he is represented? No one noble family is sprung from him.

However, not to disturb too much the erudition of those who have read the dismal story of his cruelties, and settled their ideas of his tyranny and usurpation, I declare I am not going to write a vindication of him. All I mean to show, is, that though he may have been as execrable as we are told he was, we have little or no reason to believe so. If the propensity of habit should still incline a single man to *suppose* that all he has read of Richard is true, I beg no more, than that that person would be so impartial as to own that he has little or no foundation for supposing so.

I will state the list of the crimes charged on Richard; I will specify the authorities on which he was accused; I will give a faithful account of the historians by whom he was accused; and will then examine the circumstances of each crime and each evidence; and lastly, show that some of the crimes were contrary to Richard's interest, and almost all inconsistent with probability or with dates, and some of them involved in material contradictions.

Supposed crimes of Richard the Third.

1st. His murder of Edward prince of Wales, son of Henry the Sixth.

2d. His murder of Henry the Sixth.

3d. The murder of his brother George duke of Clarence.

4th. The execution of Rivers, Gray, and Vaughan.

5th. The execution of Lord Hastings.

6th. The murder of Edward the Fifth and his brother.

7th. The murder of his own queen.

To which may be added, as they are thrown into the list to blacken him, his intended match with his own niece Elizabeth, the penance of Jane Shore, and his own personal deformities.

I. Of the murder of Edward prince of Wales, son of Henry the Sixth.

Edward the Fourth had indubitably the hereditary right to the crown; which he pursued with singular bravery and address, and with all the arts of a politician and the cruelty of a conqueror. Indeed on neither side do there seem to have been any scruples: Yorkists and Lancastrians, Edward and Margaret of Anjou, entered into any engagements, took any oaths, violated them, and indulged their revenge, as often as they were depressed or victorious. After the battle of Tewksbury, in which Margaret and her son were made prisoners, young Edward was brought to the presence of Edward the Fourth; "but after the king," says Fabian, the oldest historian of those times, "had questioned with the said Sir Edwarde, and he had answered unto hym contrary his pleasure, he then strake him with his gauntlet upon the face; after which stroke, so by him received, he was by the kynges servants incontinently slaine." The chronicle of Croyland of the same date says, the

13

prince was slain "ultricibus quorundam manibus;" but names nobody.

Hall, who closes his work with the reign of Henry the Eighth, says, that "the prince beyinge bold of stomache and of a good courage, answered the king's question (of how he durst so presumptuously enter into his realme with banner displayed) saiynge, to recover my father's kingdome and enheritage, &c. at which wordes kyng Edward said nothing, but with his hand thrust him from him, or, as some say, stroke him with his gauntlet, whome incontinent, they that stode about, which were George duke of Clarence, Richard duke of Gloucester, Thomas marques Dorset (son of queen Elizabeth Widville) and William lord Hastynges, sodainly murthered and pitously manquelled." Thus much had the story gained from the time of Fabian to that of Hall.

Hollingshed repeats these very words, consequently is a transcriber and no new authority.

John Stowe reverts to Fabian's account, as the only one not grounded on hear-say, and affirms no more, than that the king cruelly smote the young prince on the face with his gauntlet, and after his servants slew him.

Of modern historians, Rapin and Carte, the only two who seem not to have swallowed implicitly all the vulgar tales propagated by the Lancastrians to blacken the house of York, warn us to read with allowance the exaggerated relations of those times.* The latter suspects, that at the dissolution of the monasteries all evidences were suppressed that tended to weaken the right of the prince on the throne; but as Henry the Eighth concentred in himself both the claim of Edward the Fourth and that ridiculous one of Henry the Seventh, he seems to have had less occasion to be anxious lest the truth should come out; and indeed his father had involved that truth in so much darkness, that it was little likely to force its way. Nor was it necessary then to load the memory of Richard the Third, who had left no offspring. Henry the Eighth had no competitor to fear but the descendants of Clarence, of whom he seems to have had sufficient apprehension, as appeared by his murder of the old countess of Salisbury, daughter of Clarence, and his endeavours to root out her posterity. This jealousy accounts for Hall charging the duke of Clarence, as well as the duke of Gloucester, with the murder of prince Edward. But in accusations of so deep a dye, it is not sufficient ground for our belief, that an historian reports them with such a frivolous palliative as that phrase, *as some say*. A cotemporary names the king's *servants* as perpetrators of the murder: Is not that more probable, than that the king's own brothers should have dipped their hands in so foul an assassination?* Richard, in particular, is allowed on all hands to have been a brave and martial prince: he had great share in the victory at Tewkesbury: Some years afterwards, he commanded his brother's troops in Scotland, and made himself master of Edinburgh. At the battle of Bosworth, where he fell, his courage was heroic: he fought Richmond, and endeavoured to decide their quarrel by a personal combat, slaying Sir William Brandon, his rival's standard-bearer, with his own hand, and felling to the ground Sir John Cheney, who endeavoured to oppose his fury. Such men may be carried by ambition to command the execution of those who stand in their way; but are not likely to lend their hand, in cold blood, to a base, and, to themselves, useless assassination. How did it import Richard in what manner the young prince was put to death? If he had so early planned the ambitious designs ascribed to him, he might have trusted to his brother Edward, so much more immediately concerned, that the young prince would not be spared. If those views did not, as is probable, take root in his heart till long afterwards, what interest had Richard to murder an unhappy young prince? This crime therefore was so unnecessary, and is so far from being established by any authority, that he deserves to be entirely acquitted of it.*

II. The murder of Henry the Sixth.

This charge, no better supported than the preceding, is still more improbable. "Of the death of this prince, Henry the Sixth," says Fabian, "divers tales were told. But the most common fame went, that he was sticken with a dagger by the handes of the duke of Gloceter."
The author of the Continuation of the Chronicle of Croyland says only, that the body of king Henry was found lifeless (exanime) in the Tower. "Parcat Deus", adds he, "& spatium poenitentiae Ei donet, *Quicunque* sacrilegas manus in Christum Domini ausus est immittere. Unde et agens tyranni, patiensque gloriosi martyris titulum mereatur." The prayer for the murderer, that he may live to repent, proves that the passage was written immediately after the murder was committed. That the assassin deserved the appellation of tyrant, evinces that

16

the historian's suspicions went high; but as he calls him *Quicunque*, and as we are uncertain whether he wrote before the death of Edward the Fourth or between his death and that of Richard the Third, we cannot ascertain which of the brothers he meant. In strict construction he should mean Edward, because as he is speaking of Henry's death, Richard, then only duke of Gloucester, could not properly be called a tyrant. But as monks were not good grammatical critics, I shall lay no stress on this objection. I do think he alluded to Richard; having treated him severely in the subsequent part of his history, and having a true monkish partiality to Edward, whose cruelty and vices he slightly noticed, in favour to that monarch's severity to heretics and ecclesiastic expiations. "Is princeps, licet diebus suis cupiditatibus & luxui nimis intemperanter indulsisse credatur, in fide tamen catholicus summ, hereticorum severissimus hostis, sapientium & doctorum hominum clericorumque promotor amantissimus, sacramentorum ecclesiae devotissimus ven erator, peccatorumque fuorum omnium paenit ntissimus fuit." That monster Philip the Second possessed just the same virtues. Still, I say, let the monk suspect whom he would, if Henry was found dead, the monk was not likely to know who murdered him – and if he did, he has not told us.

Hall says, "Poore kyng Henry the Sixte, a little before deprived of hys realme and imperial croune, was now in the Tower of London spoyled of his life and all wordly felicite by Richard duke of Gloucester (as the constant fame ranne) which, to thintent that king Edward his brother should be clere out of al secret suspicyon of sudden invasion, murthered the said king with a dagger." Whatever Richard was, it seems he was a most excellent and kind-hearted brother, and scrupled not on any occasion to be the Jack Ketch of the times. We shall see him soon (if the evidence were to be believed) perform the same friendly office for Edward on their brother Clarence. And we must admire that he, whose dagger was so fleshed in murder for the service of another, should be so put to it to find the means of making away with his nephews, whose deaths were considerably more essential to him. But can this accusation be allowed gravely? If Richard aspired to the crown, whose whole conduct during Edward's reign was a scene, as we are told, of plausibility and decorum, would he officiously and unnecessarily have taken on himself the odium of slaying a saint-like monarch, adored by the people? Was it his interest to save Edward's character at the expence of his own? Did Henry stand in *his* way, deposed, imprisoned, and now *childless*? The blind and indiscriminate zeal with which every crime committed in that bloody age was placed to Richard's account, makes it greatly probable, that interest of party had more hand than truth in drawing his picture. Other cruelties, which I shall mention, and to which we know his motives, he certainly commanded; nor am I desirous to purge him where I find him guilty: but mob-stories or Lancastrian forgeries ought to be rejected from sober history; nor can they be repeated, without exposing the writer to the imputation of weakness and vulgar credulity.*

III. The murder of his brother Clarence.

In the examination of this article, I shall set aside our historians (whose gossipping narratives, as we have seen, deserve little regard) because we have better authority to direct our inquiries: and this is, the attainder of the duke of Clarence, as it is set forth in the Parliamentary History (copied indeed from Habington's Life of Edward the Fourth) and by the editors of that history justly supposed to be taken from Stowe, who had seen the original bill of attainder. The crimes and conspiracy of Clarence are there particularly enumerated, and even his dealing with conjurers and necromancers, a charge however absurd, yet often made use of in that age. Eleanor Cobham, wife of Humphrey duke of Gloucester, had been condemned on a parallel accusation. In France it was a common charge; and I think, so late as in the reign of Henry the Eighth, Edward duke of Buckingham was said to have consulted astrologers and such like cattle, on the succession of the crown. Whether Clarence was guilty we cannot easily tell; for in those times neither the public nor the prisoner were often favoured with knowing the evidence on which sentence was passed. Nor was much information of that sort given to or asked by parliament itself, previous to bills of attainder. The duke of Clarence appears to have been at once a weak, volatile, injudicious, and ambitious man. He had abandoned his brother Edward, had espoused the daughter of Warwick, the great enemy of their house, and had even been declared successor to Henry the Sixth and his son prince Edward. Conduct so absurd must have left lasting impressions on Edward's mind, not to be effaced by Clarence's subsequent treachery to Henry and Warwick. The Chronicle of Croyland mentions the ill-humour and discontents of Clarence; and all our authors agree, that he kept no terms with the queen and her relations. [1] Habington adds, that these

1. That chronicle, which now-and-then, though seldom, is circumstantial, gives a curious account of the marriage of Richard duke of Gloucester and Anne Nevil, which I have found in no other author; and which seems to tax the envy and rapaciousness of Clarence as the causes of the dissention between the brothers. This account, and from a cotemporary, is the more remarkable, as the Lady Anne is positively said to have been only *betrothed* to Edward prince of Wales, son of Henry the Sixth, and not his widow, as she is carelessly called by all our historians, and represented in Shakespeare's masterly scene.* "Postquam filius regis Henrici, cui Domina Anna, minor filia comitis Warwici, *desponsata* fuit, in prefato bello de Tewkysbury occubuit," Richard duke of Gloucester desired her for his wife. Clarence, who had married the elder sister, was unwilling to share so rich an inheritance with his brother, and concealed the young lady. Gloucester was too alert for him, and discovered the Lady Anne in the dress of a cook-maid in London, and removed her to the sanctuary of St. Martin. The brothers pleaded each his cause in person before their elder brother in council; and every man, says the author, admired the strength of their respective arguments. The king composed their differences, bestowed the maiden on Gloucester, and parted the estate between him and Clarence; the countess of Warwick, mother of the heiresses, and who had brought that vast wealth to the house of Nevil, remaining the only sufferer, being reduced to a state of absolute necessity, as appears from Dugdale. In such times, under such despotic dispensations, the greatest crimes were only consequences of the œconomy of government.

discontents were secretly fomented by the duke of Gloucester. Perhaps they were: Gloucester certainly kept fair with the queen, and profited largely by the forfeiture of his brother. But where jealousies are secretly fomented in a court, they seldom come to the knowledge of an historian; and though he may have guessed right from collateral circumstances, these insinuations are mere *gratis dicta*, and can only be treated as surmises.[2] Hall, Hollingshed, and Stowe say not a word of Richard being the person who put the sentence in execution; but, on the contrary, they all say he openly resisted the murder of Clarence:* all too record another circumstance, which is perfectly ridiculous, that Clarence was drowned in a barrel or butt of malmsey. Whoever can believe that a butt of wine was the engine of his death, may believe that Richard helped him into it, and kept him down till he was suffocated. But the strong evidence on which Richard must be acquitted,

– Note, that Sir Richard Baker is so absurd as to make Richard espouse the Lady Anne after his accession, though he had a son by her ten years old at that time.

2. The chronicle above quoted asserts, that the speaker of the house of commons demanded the execution of Clarence. Is it credible that, on a proceeding so public and so solemn for that age, the brother of the offended monarch and of the royal criminal should have been deputed, or would have stooped to so vile an office? On such occasions do arbitrary princes want tools? Was Edward's court so virtuous or so humane, that it could furnish no assassin but the first prince of the blood? When the house of commons undertook to colour the king's resentment, was every member of it too scrupulous to lend his hand to the deed?

and indeed even of having contributed to his death, was the testimony of Edward himself. Being some time afterward sollicited to pardon a notorious criminal, the king's conscience broke forth; "Unhappy brother!" cried he, "for whom no man would interceed – yet ye all can be intercessors for a villain!" If Richard had been instigator or executioner, it is not likely that the king would have assumed the whole merciless criminality to himself, without bestowing a due share on his brother Gloucester. Is it possible to renew the charge, and not recollect this acquittal!

The three preceding accusations are evidently uncertain and improbable. What follows is more obscure; and it is on the ensuing transactions that I venture to pronounce, that we have little or no authority on which to form positive conclusions. I speak more particularly of the deaths of Edward the Fifth and his brother.* It will, I think, appear very problematic whether they were murdered or not: and even if they were murdered, it is impossible to believe the account as fabricated and divulged by Henry the Seventh, on whose testimony the murder must rest at last; for they, who speak most positively, revert to the story which he was pleased to publish eleven years after their supposed deaths, and which is so absurd, so incoherent, and so repugnant to dates and other facts, that as it is no longer necessary to pay court to his majesty, it is no longer necessary not to treat his assertions as an impudent fiction. I come directly to this point, because the intervening articles of the executions of Rivers, Gray, Vaughan, and Hastings will naturally find their place in that disquisition.

And here it will be important to examine those historians on whose relation the story first depends. Previous to this I must ascertain one or two dates, for they are stubborn evidence and cannot be rejected: they exist every where, and cannot be proscribed even from a Court Calendar.

Edward the Fourth died April 9th 1483.
Edward, his eldest son, was then thirteen years of age.
Richard, duke of York, his second son, was about nine.*

We have but two cotemporary historians, the author of the Chronicle of Croyland, and John Fabian.* The first, who wrote in his convent, and only mentioned incidentally affairs of state, is very barren and concise: he appears indeed not to have been ill informed, and sometimes even in a situation of personally knowing the transactions of the times; for in one place we are told in a marginal note, that the doctor of the canon law, and one of the king's councillors, who was sent to Calais, was the author of the Continuation. Whenever therefore his assertions are positive, and not merely flying reports, he ought to be admitted as fair evidence, since we have no better. And yet a monk who busies himself in recording the insignificant events of his own order or monastery, and who was at most occasionally made use of, was not likely to know the most important and most mysterious secrets of state; I mean, as he was not employed in those iniquitous transactions – if he had been, we should learn or might expect still less truth from him.*

John Fabian was a merchant, and had been sheriff of London, and died in 1512: he consequently lived on the spot at that very interesting period. Yet no sheriff was ever less qualified to write a history of England. His narrative is dry, uncircumstantial, and unimportant: he mentions the deaths of princes and revolutions of government, with the same phlegm and brevity as he would speak of the appointment of church-wardens. I say not this from any partiality, or to decry the simple man as crossing my opinion; for Fabian's testimony is far from bearing hard against Richard, even though he wrote under Henry the Seventh, who would have suffered no apology for his rival, and whose reign was employed not only in extirpating the house of York, but in forging the most atrocious calumnies to blacken their memories, and invalidate their just claim.

But the great source from whence all later historians have taken their materials for the reign of Richard the Third, is Sir Thomas More. Grafton, the next in order, has copied him verbatim: so does Hollingshed – and we are told by the former in a marginal note, that Sir Thomas was under-sheriff of London when he composed his work. It is in truth a composition, and a very beautiful one. He was then in the vigour of his fancy, and fresh from the study of the Greek and Roman historians, whose manner he has imitated in divers imaginary orations.* They serve to lengthen an unknown history of little more than two months into a pretty sizeable volume; but are no more to be received as genuine, than the facts they are adduced to countenance. An under-sheriff of London, aged but twenty-eight, and recently marked with the displeasure of the crown, was not likely to be furnished with materials from any high authority, and could not receive them from the best authority, I mean the adverse party, who were proscribed, and all their chiefs banished or put to death. Let us again recur to dates.[3] Sir Thomas More was born in 1480: he was appointed under-sheriff in 1508, and three years before had offended Henry the Seventh in the tender point of opposing a subsidy. Buck, the apologist of Richard the Third, ascribes the authorities of Sir Thomas to the information of archbishop Morton; and it is true that he had been brought up under that prelate; but Morton died in 1500, when Sir Thomas was but twenty years old, and when he had scarce thought of writing history. What materials he had gathered from his master were probably nothing more than a general narrative of the preceding times in discourse at dinner or in a winter's evening, if so raw a youth can be supposed to have been admitted to familiarity with a prelate of that rank and prime minister. But granting that such pregnant parts as More's had leaped the barrier of dignity, and insinuated himself into the archbishop's favour; could he have drawn from a more corrupted source? Morton had not only violated his allegiance to Richard; but had been the chief engine to dethrone him, and to plant a bastard scyon in the throne. Of all men living there could not be more suspicious testimony than the prelate's, except the king's: and had the archbishop selected More for the historian of those dark scenes, who had so much interest to blacken Richard, as the man who had

3.   Vide Biog. Britannica, p. 3159.

risen to be prime minister to his rival? Take it therefore either way; that the archbishop did or did not pitch on a young man of twenty to write that history, his authority was as suspicious as could be.

It may be said, on the other hand, that Sir Thomas, who had smarted for his boldness (for his father, a judge of the king's bench, had been imprisoned and fined for his son's offence) had had little inducement to flatter the Lancastrian cause. It is very true; nor am I inclined to impute adulation to one of the honestest statesmen and brightest names in our annals. He who scorned to save his life by bending to the will of the son, was not likely to canvass the favour of the father, by prostituting his pen to the humour of the court. I take the truth to be, that Sir Thomas wrote his reign of Edward the Fifth as he wrote his Utopia; to amuse his leisure and exercise his fancy. He took up a paltry canvas and embroidered it with a flowing design as his imagination suggested the colours. I should deal more severely with his respected memory on any other hypothesis. He has been guilty of such palpable and material falshoods, as, while they destroy his credit as an historian, would reproach his veracity as a man, if we could impute them to premeditated perversion of truth, and not to youthful levity and inaccuracy. Standing as they do, the sole groundwork of that reign's history, I am authorized to pronounce the work, invention and romance.

Polidore Virgil, a foreigner, and author of a light Latin history, was here during the reigns of Henry the Seventh and Eighth. I may quote him now-and-then, and the Chronicle of Croyland; but neither furnish us with much light.

There was another foreign writer in that age of far greater authority, whose negligent simplicity and veracity are unquestionable; who had great opportunities of knowing our story, and whose testimony is corroborated by our records: I mean Philip de Comines. He and Buck agree with one another, and with the rolls of parliament; Sir Thomas More with none of them.

Buck, so long exploded as a lover of paradoxes, and as an advocate for a monster, gains new credit the deeper this dark scene is fathomed. Undoubtedly Buck has gone too far; nor are his style or method to be admired. With every intention of vindicating Richard, he does but authenticate his crimes, by searching in other story for parallel instances of what he calls policy.

No doubt politicians will acquit Richard, if confession of his crimes be pleaded in defence of them. Policy will justify his taking off opponents. Policy will maintain him in removing those who would have barred his obtaining the crown, whether he thought he had a right to it, or was determined to obtain it. Morality, especially in the latter case, cannot take his part. I shall speak more to this immediately. Rapin conceived doubts; but instead of pursuing them, wandered after judgments; and they will lead a man where-ever he has a mind to be led. Carte, with more manly shrewdness, has sifted many parts of Richard's story, and guessed happily. My part has less penetration; but the parliamentary history, the comparison of dates, and the authentic monument lately come to light, and from which I shall give extracts, have convinced me, that, if Buck is too favourable, all our other historians

27

are blind guides, and have not made out a twentieth part of their assertions.

The story of Edward the Fifth is thus related by Sir Thomas More, and copied from him by all our historians.

When the king his father died, the prince kept his court at Ludlow, under the tuition of his maternal uncle Anthony earl Rivers. Richard duke of Gloucester was in the north, returning from his successful expedition against the Scots. The queen wrote instantly to her brother to bring up the young king to London, with a train of two thousand horse: a fact allowed by historians, and which, whether a prudent caution or not, was the first overt-act of the new reign; and likely to strike, as it did strike, the duke of Gloucester and the antient nobility with a jealousy, that the queen intended to exclude them from the administration, and to govern in concert with her own family. It is not improper to observe that no precedent authorized her to assume such power. Joan, princess dowager of Wales, and widow of the Black Prince, had no share in the government during the minority of her son Richard the Second. Catherine of Valois, widow of Henry the Fifth, was alike excluded from the regency, though her son was but a year old. And if Isabella governed on the deposition of Edward the Second, it was by an usurped power, by the same power that had contributed to dethrone her husband; a power sanctified by no title, and confirmed by no act of parliament.[4] The first

4. Twelve guardians were appointed by parliament, and the earl of Lancaster was entrusted with the care of the king's person. The latter, being ex-

step to a female regency[5] enacted, though it never took place, was many years afterwards, in the reign of Henry the Eighth.

Edward, on his death-bed, had patched up a reconciliation between his wife's kindred and the great lords of the court; particularly between the marquis Dorset, the queen's son, and the lord chamberlain Hastings. Yet whether the disgusted lords had only seemed to yield, to satisfy the dying king, or whether the steps taken by the queen gave them new cause of umbrage, it appears that the duke of Buckingham was the first to communicate his suspicions to Gloucester, and to dedicate himself to his service. Lord Hastings was scarce less forward to join in like measures: and all three, it is pretended, were so alert, that they contrived to have it insinuated to the queen, that it would give much offence if the young king should be brought to London with so great a force as she had ordered; on which suggestions she wrote to Lord Rivers to countermand her first directions.

It is difficult not to suspect, that our historians have imagined more plotting in this transaction than could easily be compassed in so short a period, and in an age when no communication could be carried on but by special messengers, in bad roads, and with no relays of post-horses.

Edward the Fourth died April 9th, and his

cluded from exercising his charge by the queen and Mortimer, gave that as a reason for not obeying a summons to parliament. Vide Parliam. Hist. vol. i, p. 208. 215.

5. Vide the act of succession in Parl. Hist. vol. iii. p. 127.

son made his entrance into London[6] May 4th. * It is not probable, that the queen communicated her directions for bringing up her son with an armed force to the lords of the council, and her newly reconciled enemies. But she might be betrayed. Still it required some time for Buckingham to send his servant Percival (though Sir Thomas More vaunts his expedition) to York, where the duke of Gloucester then lay;[7] for Percival's return (it must be observed too that the duke of Buckingham was in Wales, consequently did not learn the queen's orders on the spot, but either received the account from London, or learnt it from Ludlow); for the two dukes to send instructions to their confederates in London; for the impression to be made on the queen, and for her dispatching her counter-orders; for Percival to post back and meet Gloucester at Nottingham, and for returning thence and bringing his master Buckingham to meet Richard at Northampton, at the very time of the king's arrival there. All this might happen, undoubtedly; and yet who will believe, that such mysterious and rapid negociations came to the knowledge of Sir Thomas More

6. Fabian.
7. It should be remarked too, that the duke of Gloucester is positively said to be celebrating his brother's obsequies there. It not only strikes off part of the term by allowing the necessary time for the news of king Edward's death to reach York, and for the preparations to be made there to solemnize a funeral for him; but this very circumstance takes off from the probability of Richard having as yet laid any plan for dispossessing his nephew. Would he have loitered at York at such a crisis, if he had intended to step into the throne?

twenty-five years afterwards, when, as it will appear, he knew nothing of very material and public facts that happened at the same period?

But whether the circumstances are true, or whether artfully imagined, it is certain that the king, with a small force, arrived at Northampton, and thence proceeded to Stony Stratford. Earl Rivers remained at Northampton, where he was cajoled by the two dukes till the time of rest, when the gates of the inn were suddenly locked, and the earl made prisoner. Early in the morning the two dukes hastened to Stony Stratford, where, in the king's presence, they picked a quarrel with his other half-brother, the lord Richard Grey, accusing him, the marquis Dorset, and their uncle Rivers, of ambitious and hostile designs, to which ends the marquis had entered the Tower, taken treasure thence, and sent a force to sea.

"These things," says Sir Thomas, *"the dukes knew were done for good and necessary purposes, and by appointment of the council; but somewhat they must say."* As Sir Thomas has not been pleased to specify those purposes, and as in those times at least privy councellors were exceedingly complaisant to the ruling powers, he must allow us to doubt whether the purposes of the queen's relations were quite so innocent as he would make us believe; and whether the princes of the blood and the ancient nobility had not some reason to be jealous that the queen was usurping more power than the laws had given her. The catastrophe of her whole family so truly deserves commiseration, that we are apt to shut our eyes to all her weakness and ill-judged policy; and yet at every step we find how much she contributed to draw ruin on their heads and her own,

31

by the confession even of her apologists. The duke of Gloucester was the first prince of the blood, the constitution pointed him out as regent; no will, no disposition of the late king was even alledged to bar his pretensions; he had served the state with bravery, success, and fidelity; and the queen herself, who had been insulted by Clarence, had had no cause to complain of Gloucester. Yet all her conduct intimated designs of governing by force in the name of her son.[8] If these facts are impartially stated, and grounded on the confession of those who enveigh most bitterly against Richard's memory, let us allow that at least *thus far* he acted as most princes would have done in his situation, in a lawless and barbarous age; and rather instigated by others, than from any before-conceived ambition and system. If the journeys of Percival are true, Buckingham was the devil that tempted Richard; and if Richard

8. Grafton says, "and in effect every one as he was neerest of kinne unto the queene, so was he planted nere about the prince," p. 761; and again, p. 762, "the duke of Gloucester understanding that the lordes, which were about the king, entended to bring him up to his coronation, accompanied with such power of their friendes, that it should be hard for him, to bring his purpose to passe, without gatherying and assemble of people, and in manner of open war," &c. In the same place it appears, that the argument used to dissuade the queen from employing force, was, that it would be a breach of the accommodation made by the late king between her relations and the great lords; and so un-doubtedly it was; and though they are accused of violating the epace, it is plain that the queen's insincerity had been at least equal to theirs, and that the infringement of the reconciliation commenced on her side.

still wanted instigation, then it must follow, that he had not murdered Henry the Sixth, his son, and Clarence, to pave his own way to the crown. If this fine story of Buckingham and Percival is not true, what becomes of Sir Thomas More's credit, on which the whole fabric leans?

Lord Richard, Sir Thomas Vaughan, and Sir Richard Hawte, were arrested, and with lord Rivers sent prisoners to Pomfret, while the dukes conducted the king by easy stages to London.

The queen, hearing what had happened, took sanctuary at Westminster, with her other son the duke of York, and the princesses her daughters. Rotheram, archbishop of York and Lord Chancellor, repaired to her with the great seal, and endeavoured to comfort her dismay with a friendly message he had received from Hastings, who was with the confederate lords on the road.* "A woe worth him!" quoth the queen, "for *it is he* that goeth about to destroy me and my blood!" Not a word is said of her suspecting the duke of Gloucester. The archbishop seems to have been the first who entertained any suspicion; and yet, if all that our historian says of him is true, Rotheram was far from being a shrewd man: witness the indiscreet answer which he is said to have made on this occasion. "Madam," quoth he, "be of good comfort, and assure you, if they crown any other king than your son whom they now have, we shall on the morrow crown his brother, whom you have here with you." Did the silly prelate think that it would be much consolation to a mother, whose eldest son might be murdered, that her younger son would be crowned in prison! or was she to be satisfied with seeing one son entitled to the crown, and the other enjoying it nominally?

He then delivered the seal to the queen, and as lightly sent for it back immediately after.

The dukes continued their march, declaring they were bringing the king to his coronation. Hastings, who seems to have preceded them, endeavoured to pacify the apprehensions which had been raised in the people, acquainting them that the arrested lords had been imprisoned for plotting against the dukes of Gloucester and Buckingham. As both those princes were of the blood royal,[9] this accusation was not ill founded, it having evidently been the intention, as I have shewn, to bar them from any share in the administration, to which, by the custom of the realm, they were intitled. So much depends on this foundation, that I shall be excused from enforcing it. The queen's party were the aggressors; and though that alone would not justify all

9.   Henry duke of Buckingham was the immediate descendant and heir of Thomas of Woodstock duke of Gloucester, the youngest son of Edward the Third, as will appear by this table:

```
          Thomas
       duke of Gloucester
            |
          Anne ———————┬——Edmund earl of Stafford
       sole dr. and heiress  |
            Humphrey duke of Bucks
                   |
            Humphrey lord Stafford
                   |
            Henry duke of Bucks
```

It is plain, that Buckingham was influenced by this nearness to the crown, for it made him overlook his own alliance with the queen, whose sister he had married. Henry the Eighth did not overlook the proximity of blood, when he afterwards put to death the son of this duke.

the following excesses, yet we must not judge of those times by the present. Neither the crown nor the great men were restrained by sober established forms and proceedings as they are at present; and from the death of Edward the Third, force alone had dictated. Henry the Fourth had stepped into the throne contrary to all justice. A title so defective had opened a door to attempts as violent; and the various innovations introduced in the latter years of Henry the Sixth had annihilated all ideas of order. Richard duke of York had been declared successor to the crown during the life of Henry and of his son prince Edward, and, as appears by the Parliamentary History, though not noticed by our careless historians, was even appointed prince of Wales. The duke of Clarence had received much such another declaration in his favour during the short restoration of Henry. What temptations were these precedents to an affronted prince! We shall see soon what encouragement they gave him to examine closely into his nephew's pretensions; and how imprudent it was in the queen to provoke Gloucester, when her very existence as queen was liable to strong objections. Nor ought the subsequent executions of Lord Rivers, Lord Richard Grey, and of Lord Hastings himself, to be considered in so very strong a light, as they would appear in, if acted in modern times. During the wars of York and Lancaster, no forms of trial had been observed. Not only peers taken in battle had been put to death without process; but whoever, though not in arms, was made prisoner by the victorious party, underwent the same fate; as was the case of Tiptoft earl of Worcester, who had fled and was taken in disguise. Trials had never been used with any degree of strictness, as at present; and though Richard was pursued and killed as an usurper, the Solomon that succeeded him, was not a jot less a tyrant. Henry the Eighth was still less of a temper to give greater latitude to the laws. In fact, little ceremony or judicial proceeding was observed on trials, till the reign of Elizabeth, who, thought decried of late for her despotism, in order to give some shadow of countenance to the tyranny of the Stuarts, was the first of our princes, under whom any gravity or equity was allowed in cases of treason. To judge impartially therefore, we ought to recall the temper and manners of the times we read of. It is shocking to eat our enemies; but it is not so shocking in an Iroquois, as it would be in the king of Prussia. And this is all I contend for, that the crimes of Richard, which he really committed, at least which we have reason to believe he committed, were more the crimes of the age than of the man; and except these executions of Rivers, Grey, and Hastings, I defy any body to prove one other of those charged to his account, from any good authority.

It is alledged that the partizans of Gloucester strictly guarded the sanctuary, to prevent farther resort thither; but Sir Thomas confesses too, that *divers lords, knights, and gentlemen, either for favour of the queen, or for fear of themselves, assembled companies, and went flocking together in harness.* Let us strip this paragraph of its historic buskins, and it is plain that *the queen's party took up arms.* [10]* This is no indifferent circumstance.

10.   This is confirmed by the chronicle of Croyland, p. 566.

She had plotted to keep possession of the king, and to govern in his name by force, but had been outwitted, and her family had been imprisoned for the attempt. Conscious that she was discovered, perhaps reasonably alarmed at Gloucester's designs, she had secured herself and her younger children in sanctuary. Necessity rather than law justified her proceedings, – but what excuse can be made for her faction having recourse to arms? who was authorized, by the tenour of former reigns, to guard the king's person, till parliament should declare a regency, but his uncle and the princes of the blood? endeavouring to establish the queen's authority by force was rebellion against the laws. I state this minutely, because the fact has never been attended to; and later historians pass it over, as if Richard had hurried on the deposition of his nephews without any colour of decency, and without the least provocation to any of his proceedings. Hastings is even said to have warned the citizens that matters were likely *to come to a field* (to a battle) from the opposition of the adverse party, though as yet no symptom had appeared of designs against the king, whom the two dukes were bringing to his coronation. Nay, it is not probable that Gloucester had as yet meditated more than securing the regency; for had he had designs on the crown, would he have weakened his own claim by assuming the protectorate, which he could not accept but by acknowledging the title of his nephew? This in truth seems to me to have been the case. The ambition of the queen and her family alarmed the princes and the nobility: Gloucester, Buckingham, Hastings, and many more had checked those attempts.

The next step was to secure the regency: but none of these acts could be done without grievous provocation to the queen. As soon as her son should come of age, she might regain her power and the means of revenge. Self-security prompted the princes and lords to guard against this reverse, and what was equally dangerous to the queen, the depression of her fortune called forth and revived all the hatred of her enemies.

Her marriage had given universal offence to the nobility, and been the source of all the late disturbances and bloodshed. The great earl of Warwick, provoked at the contempt shewn to him by king Edward while negotiating a match for him in France, had abandoned him for Henry the Sixth, whom he had again set on the throne. These calamities were still fresh in every mind, and no doubt contributed to raise Gloucester to the throne, which he could not have attained without almost general concurrence: yet if we are to believe historians, he, Buckingham, the mayor of London, and one Dr. Shaw, operated this revolution by a sermon and a speech to the people, though the people would not even give a huzza to the proposal. The change of government in the Rehearsal is not effected more easily by the physician and gentleman usher,

Do you take this, and I'll seize t'other chair.

In what manner Richard assumed or was invested with the protectorate does not appear. Sir Thomas More, speaking of him by that title, says, "the protector which always you must take for the duke of Gloucester," Fabian after men-

38

tioning the solemn[11] arrival of the king in London, adds, "Than provisyon was made for the kinge's coronation; in which pastime (interval) the duke being admitted for lord protectour." As the parliament was not sitting, this dignity was no doubt conferred on him by the assent of the lords and privy council; and as we hear of no opposition, none was probably made. He was the only person to whom that rank was due; his right could not and does not seem to have been questioned. The Chronicle of Croyland corroborates my opinion, saying, "Accepitque dictus Ricardus dux Glocestriae illum solennem magistratum, qui duci Humfrido Glocestriae, stante minore aetate regis Henrici, ut regni protector appellaretur, olim contingebat. Eâ igitur auctoritate usus est, de consensu & beneplacito *omnium dominorum*," p. 556.

Thus far therefore it must be allowed that Richard acted no illegal part, nor discovered more ambition than became him. He had defeated the queen's innovations, and secured her accomplices. To draw off our attention from such regular steps, Sir Thomas More has exhaulted all his eloquence and imagination to work up a piteous scene, in which the queen is made to excite our compassion in the highest degree, and is furnished by that able pen with strains of pathetic oratory, which no part of her

11.   He was probably eye-witness of that ceremony; for he says, "the king was of the maior and his citizens met at Harnesey parke, the maior and his brethren being clothed in scarlet, and the citizens in violet, to the number of V.C. horses, and than from thence conveyed unto the citie, the king beynge in blewe velvet, and all his lords and servauntes in blacke cloth.   p. 513.

conduct affords us reason to believe she possessed. This scene is occasioned by the demand of delivering up her second son. Cardinal Bourchier archbishop of Canterbury is the instrument employed by the protector to effect this purpose. The fact is confirmed by Fabian in his rude and brief manner, and by the Chronicle of Croyland, and therefore cannot be disputed. But though the latter author affirms, that force was used to oblige the cardinal to take that step, he by no means agrees with Sir Thomas More in the repugnance of the queen to comply, nor in that idle discussion on the privileges of sanctuaries, on which Sir Thomas has wasted so many words. On the contrary, the chronicle declares, that the queen "Verbis gratanter annuens, dimisit puerum." The king, who had been lodged in the palace of the bishop of London, was now removed with his brother to the Tower.

This last circumstance has not a little contributed to raise horror in vulgar minds, who of late years have been accustomed to see no persons of rank lodged in the Tower but state criminals. But in that age the case was widely different. It not only appears by a map engraven so late as the reign of queen Elizabeth, that the Tower was a royal palace, in which were ranges of buildings called the king's and queen's apartments, now demolished; but it is a known fact, that they did often lodge there, especially previous to their coronations. The queen of Henry the Seventh lay in there: queen Elizabeth went thither after her triumphant entry into the city; and many other instances might be produced, but for brevity I omit them, to come to one of the principal transactions of this dark period: I mean Richard's assumption of the crown. Sir Thomas More's account of this extraordinary event is totally improbable, and positively false in the ground-work of that revolution. He tells us, that Richard meditating usurpation, divided the lords into two separate councils, assembling the king's or queen's party at Baynard's castle, but holding his own private junto at Crosby Place. From the latter he began with spreading murmurs, whispers, and reports against the legality of the late king's marriage. – Thus far we may credit him – but what man of common sense can believe, that Richard went so far as publicly to asperse the honour of his own mother? That mother, Cecily duchess dowager of York, a princess of a spotless character, was then living: so were two of her daughters, the duchesses of Suffolk and Burgundy, Richard's own sisters: one of them, the duchess of Suffolk walked at his ensuing coronation, and her son the earl of Lincoln was by Richard himself, after the death of his own son, declared heir apparent to the crown. Is it, can it be credible, that Richard actuated a venal[12] preacher to declare to the people from the pulpit at Paul's cross, that his mother had been an adulteress, and that her

12.   What should we think of a modern historian, who should sink all mention of the convention parliament, and only tell us that one Dr. Burnet got up into the pulpit, and assured the people that Henrietta Maria (a little more suspected of gallantry than duchess Cecily) produced Charles the Second and James the Second in adultery, and gave no legitimate issue to Charles the First, but Mary princess of Orange, mother of king William; that the people laughed at him, and so the prince of Orange became king?

41

two eldest sons,[13] Edward the Fourth and the duke of Clarence[14] were spurious; and that the good lady had not given a legitimate child to her husband, but the protector, and I suppose the duchess of Suffolk, though no mention is said to be made of her in the sermon? For as the duchess of Suffolk was older than Richard, and consequently would have been involved in the charge of bastardy, could he have declared her son his heir, he who set aside his brother Edward's children for their illegitimacy? Ladies of the least disputable gallantry generally suffer their husbands to beget his heir; and if doubts arise on the legitimacy of their issue, the younger branches seem most liable to suspicion – but a tale so gross could not have passed even on the mob – no proof, no presumption of the fact was pretended. Were[15] the duchess and her

13. The Earl of Rutland, another son, elder than Richard, had been murdered at the battle of Wakefield, and so was omitted in that imaginary accusation.

14. Clarence is the first who is said to have propagated this slander, and it was much more consonant to his levity and indigested politics, than to the good sense of Richard. Who can believe that Richard renewed this story, especially as he must have altered the dates of his mother's amours, and made them continue to her conception of him, as Clarence had made them stop in his own favour?

15. It appears from Rymer's Foedera, that the very first act of Richard's reign is dated from quadam alterâ camerâ juxta capellam in hospitio dominae Ceciliae ducissae Eborum. It does not look much as if he had publicly accused his mother of adultery, when he held his first council at her house. Among the Harleian MSS. in the Museum, No. 2236. art. 6.* is the following letter from Richard to this very princess his mother, which is an additional proof of

daughters silent on so scandalous an insinuation? Agrippina would scarce have heard it with patience. Moriar modo imperet! said that empress, in her wild wish of crowning her son: but had he, unprovoked, aspersed her honour in the open forum, would the mother have submitted to so unnatural an insult? In Richard's case the imputation was beyond measure atrocious and absurd. What! taint the fame of his mother to pave his way to the crown! Who had heard of her guilt? And if guilty, how came she to stop the career of her intrigues? But Richard had better pretentions, and had no occasion to start doubts even on his own legitimacy, which was too much connected with that of his brothers to be tossed and bandied about before the multitude. Clarence had been solemnly attainted by act of parliament, and his children were out of the question. The doubts on the validity of Edward's marriage were better grounds for

the good terms on which they lived: "Madam, I recomaunde me to you as hertely as is to me possible, beseching you in my most humble and affectuouse wise of your daly blessing to my synguler comfort and defence in my nede; and, madam, I hertely beseche you, that I may often here from you to my comfort; and suche newes as be here, my servaunt Thomas Bryan this berer shall showe you, to whome please it you to yeve credence unto. And, madam, I beseche you to be good and graciouse lady to my lord my chamberlayn to be your officer in Wiltshire in suche as Colinbourne had: I trust he shall therin do you good servyce; and that it plese you, that by this berer I may understande your pleasur in this behalve. And I praye God sende you th'accomplishement of your noble desires. Written at Pountfreit, the thirde day of Juyn, with the hande of your most humble son, Ricardus Rex."

43

Richard's proceedings than aspersion of his mother's honour. On that invalidity he claimed the crown, and obtained it; and with such universal concurrence, that the nation un-doubtedly was on his side — but as he could not deprive his nephews, on that foundation, with-out bastardizing their sisters too, no wonder the historians, who wrote under the Lancastrian domination, have used all their art and industry to misrepresent the fact. If the marriage of Edward the Fourth with the widow Grey was bigamy, and consequently null, what became of the title of Elizabeth of York, wife of Henry the Seventh? What became of it? Why a bastard branch of Lancaster, matched with a bastard of York, were obtruded on the nation as the right heirs of the crown; and, as far as two negatives can make an affirmative, they were so.

Buck, whose integrity will more and more appear, affirms that, before Edward had espoused the lady Grey, he had been contracted to the lady Eleanor Butler, and married to her by the bishop of Bath. Sir Thomas More, on the contrary (and here it is that I am unwillingly obliged to charge that great man with wilful falshood) pretends that the duchess of York, his mother, endeavouring to dissuade him from so disproportionate an alliance, urged him with a pre-contract to one Elizabeth Lucy, who howev-er, being pressed, confessed herself his con-cubine; but denied any marriage. Dr. Shaw too, the preacher, we are told by the same authority, pleaded from the pulpit the king's former marriage with Elizabeth Lucy; and the duke of Buckingham is said to have harangued the people to the same effect. But now let us see how the case really stood: Elizabeth Lucy was the daughter of one Wyat of Southampton, a mean gentleman, says Buck, and the wife of one Lucy, as mean a man as Wyat. The mistress of Edward she notoriously was; but what if, in Richard's pursuit of the crown, no question at all was made of this Elizabeth Lucy? We have the best and most undoubted authorities to assure us, that Edward's pre-contract or marriage, urged to invalidate his match with the lady Grey, was with the lady Eleanor Talbot, widow of the lord Butler of Sudeley, and sister of the earl of Shrewsbury, one of the greatest peers in the kingdom; her mother was the lady Katherine Stafford, daughter of Humphrey duke of Buckingham, prince of the blood: an alliance in that age never reckoned unsuitable.* Hear the evidence. Honest Philip de Comines says,[16] "that the bishop of Bath informed Richard, that he had married king Edward to an English lady; & dit cet evesque qu'il les avoit espouses, & que n'y avoit que luy & ceux deux." This is not positive, and yet the description marks out the lady Butler, and not Elizabeth Lucy. But the Chronicle of Croyland is more express. "Color autem introitus & captae possessionis hujusmodi is erat. Ostendebatur per modum supplicationis in quodam rotulo pergameni quod filii regis Edwardi erant bastardi,

16. Liv. 5. p. 151. In the 6th book, Comines insinuates that the bishop acted out of revenge for having been imprisoned by Edward: it might be so; but as Comines had before alledged that the bishop had actually said he had married them, it might be the truth that the prelate told out of revenge, and not a lie; nor is it probable that his tale would have had any weight, if false, and unsupported by other circumstances.

45

supponendo illum precontraxisse cum quâdam dominâ Alienorâ Boteler, antequam reginam Elizabeth duxisset uxorem; atque insuper, quod sanguis alterius fratris sui, Georgii ducis Clarentiae, fuisset attinctus; ita quod hodie nullus certus & incorruptus sanguis linealis ex parte Richardi ducis Eboraci poterat inveniri, nisi in personâ dicti Richardi ducis Glocestriae. Quo circa supplicabatur ei in fine ejusdem rotuli, *ex parte dominorum & communitatis regni*, ut jus suum in se assumeret." Is this full? Is this evidence? Here we see the origin of the tale relating to the duchess of York; *nullus certus & incorruptus sanguis*: from these mistaken or perverted words flowed the report of Richard's aspersing his mother's honour. But as if truth was doomed to emerge, though stifled for near three hundred years, the roll of parliament is at length come to light (with other wonderful discoveries) and sets forth, "that though *the three estates* which petitioned Richard to assume the crown were not assembled in form of parliament;"* yet it rehearses the supplication (recorded by the chronicle above) and declares, "that king Edward was and stood married and troth plight to one dame Eleanor Butler, daughter to the earl of Shrewsbury, with whom the said king Edward had made a pre-contract of matrimony, long before he made his pretended marriage with Elizabeth Grey." Could Sir Thomas More be ignorant of this fact? or, if ignorant, where is his competence as an historian? And how egregiously absurd is his romance of Richard's assuming the crown in consequence of Dr. Shaw's sermon and Buckingham's harangue, to neither of which he pretends the people assented! Dr. Shaw no doubt tapped the matter to the people; for Fabian asserts that he durst never shew his face afterwards; and as Henry the Seventh succeeded so soon, and as the slanders against Richard increased, that might happen; but it is evident that the nobility were disposed to call the validity of the queen's marriage in question, and that Richard was solemnly invited by the three estates to accept the regal dignity; and that is farther confirmed by the Chronicle of Croyland, which says, that Richard, having brought together a great force from the north, from Wales, and other parts, did on the twenty-sixth of June claim the crown, "seque eodem die apud magnam aulam Westmonasterij in cathedram marmoream ibi intrusit;" *but* the supplication afore-mentioned had first been presented to him. This will no doubt be called violence and a force laid on the three estates; and yet that appears by no means to have been the case; for Sir Thomas More, partial as he was against Richard, says, "that to be sure of all enemies, he sent for five thousand men out of the north against his coronation, which came up evill apparelled and worse harnessed, in rusty harnes- se, neither defensable nor scoured to the sale, which mustered in Finsbury field, to the great disdain of all lookers on." These rusty compan- ions, despised by the citizens, were not likely to intimidate a warlike nobility; and had force been used to extort their assent, Sir Thomas would have been the first to have told us so. But he suppressed an election that appears to have been voluntary, and invented a scene, in which, by his own account, Richard met with nothing but backwardness and silence, that amounted to a refusal. The probability therefore remains, that the nobility met Richard's claim at least half-way, from their hatred and jealousy of the queen's family, and many of them from the conviction of Edward's pre-contract. Many might concur from provocation at the attempts that had been made to disturb the due course of law, and some from apprehension of a minority. This last will appear highly probable from three striking circumstances that I shall mention hereafter. The great regularity with which the coronation was prepared and conducted, and the extraordinary concourse of the nobility at it, have not at all the air of an unwelcome revolution, accomplished merely by violence. On the contrary, it bore great resemblance to a much later event, which, being the last of the kind, we term *The Revolution*. The three estates of nobility, clergy, and people, which called Richard to the Crown, and whose act was confirmed by the subsequent parliament, trod the same steps as the convention did which elected the prince of Orange; both setting aside an illegal pretender, the legitimacy of whose birth was called in question. And though the partizans of the Stuarts may exult at my comparing king William to Richard the Third, it will be no matter of triumph, since it appears that Richard's cause was as good as king William's, and that in both instances it was a free election. The art used by Sir Thomas More (when he could not deny a pre-contract) in endeavouring to shift that objection on Elizabeth Lucy, a married woman, contrary to the specific words of the act of parliament, betrays the badness of the Lancastrian cause, which would make us doubt or wonder at the consent of the nobility in giving way to the act for bastardizing the children of Edward the Fourth. But reinstate the claim of the lady Butler, which probably was well known, and conceive the interest that her great relations must have made to set aside the queen's marriage, nothing appears more natural than Richard's succession. His usurpation vanishes, and in a few pages more, I shall shew that his consequential cruelty vanishes too, or at most is very problematic: but first I must revert to some intervening circumstances.

In this whole story nothing is less known to us than the grounds on which lord Hastings was put to death. He had lived in open enmity with the queen and her family, and had been but newly reconciled to her son the marquis Dorset; yet Sir Thomas owns that lord Hastings was one of the first to abet Richard's proceedings against her, and concurred in all the protector's measures. We are amazed therefore to find this lord the first sacrifice under the new government. Sir Thomas More supposes (and he could only suppose; for whatever archbishop Morton might tell him of the plots of Henry of Richmond, Morton was certainly not entrusted with the secrets of Richard) Sir Thomas, I say, supposes, that Hastings either withstood the deposition of Edward the Fifth, or was accused of such a design by Catesby, who was deeply in his confidence; and he owns that the protector *undoubtedly loved him well, and loth he was to have him lost*. What then is the presumption? Is it not, that Hastings really was plotting to defeat the new settlement contrary to the intention of the three estates? And who can tell whether the suddenness of the execution was not the effect of necessity? The gates of the Tower were shut during that rapid scene,* the protector and his adherents appeared in the first rusty armour that was at hand: but this circumstance is alledged against them, as an incident contrived to gain belief, as if they had been in danger of their lives. The argument is gratis dictum; and as Richard loved Hastings and had used his ministry, the probability lies on the other side: and it is more reasonable to believe that Richard acted in self-defence, than that he exercised a wanton, unnecessary, and disgusting cruelty. The collateral circumstances introduced by More do but weaken[17] his account, and take from its probability. I do not not mean the silly recapitulation of silly omens which forewarned Hastings of his fate, and as omens generally do, to no manner of purpose; but I speak of the idle accusations put into the mouth of Richard, such as his baring his withered arm, and imputing it to sorcery, and to his blending the queen and Jane Shore in the same plot. Cruel or not, Richard was no fool; and therefore it is highly

17. Except the proclamation which, Sir Thomas says, appeared to have been prepared before hand. The death of Hastings, I allow, is the fact of which we are most sure, without knowing the immediate motives: we must conclude it was determined on his opposing Richard's claim: farther we do not know, nor whether that opposition was made in a legal or hostile manner. It is impossible to believe that, an hour before his death, he should have exulted in the deaths of their common enemies, and vaunted, as Sir Thomas More asserts, his connection with Richard, if he was then actually at variance with him; nor that Richard should, without provocation, have massacred so excellent an accomplice. This story, therefore, must be left in the dark, as we find it.

improbable that he should lay the withering of his arm on recent witchcraft, if it was true, as Sir Thomas More pretends, that it never had been otherwise – but of the blemishes and deformity of his person, I shall have occasion to speak hereafter. For the other accusation of a league between Elizabeth and Jane Shore, Sir Thomas More ridicules it himself, and treats it as highly unlikely. But being unlikely, was it not more natural for him to think, that it never was urged by Richard? And though Sir Thomas again draws aside our attention by the penance of Jane, which she certainly underwent, it is no kind of proof that the protector accused the queen of having plotted[18] with mistress Shore. What relates to that unhappy fair one I shall examine at the end of this work.

The very day on which Hastings was executed, were beheaded earl Rivers, Lord Richard Grey, Vaughan, and Haute.* These executions are indubitable; were consonant to

18. So far from it, that, as Mr. Hume remarks, there is in Rymer's Foedera a proclamation of Richard, in which he accuses, not the lord Hastings, but the marquis Dorset, of connection with Jane Shore. Mr. Hume thinks so authentic a paper not sufficient to overbalance the credit due to Sir Thomas More. What little credit was due to him appears from the course of this work in various and indubitable instances. The proclamation against the lord Dorset and Jane Shore is not dated till the 23rd of October following. Is it credible that Richard would have made use of this woman's name again, if he had employed it before to blacken Hastings? It is not probable that, immediately on the death of the king, she had been taken into keeping by lord Hastings; but near seven months had elapsed between that death and her connection with the marquis.

the manners and violence of the age; and perhaps justifiable by that wicked code, state necessity. I have never pretended to deny them, because I find them fully authenticated. I have in another[19] place done justice to the virtues and excellent qualities of earl Rivers: let therefore my impartiality be believed, when I reject other facts, for which I can discover no good authority. I can have no interest in Richard's guilt or innocence; but as Henry the Seventh was so much interested to represent him as guilty, I cannot help imputing to the greater usurper, and to the worse tyrant of the two, all that appears to me to have been calumny and misrepresentation.

All obstacles thus removed, and Richard being solemnly instated in the throne by the concurrent voice of the three estates, "He openly," says Sir Thomas More, "took upon him to be king the[20] ninth day of June,* and the morrow after was proclaimed, riding to Westminster with great state; and calling the judges before him, straitly commanded them to execute the laws without favour or delay, with many good exhortations, of the which he followed not one." This is an invidious and false accusation. Richard, in his regal capacity, was an excellent king, and for the short time of his reign enacted many wise and wholesome laws. I doubt even whether one of the best proofs of his

19. In the Catalogue of Royal and Noble Authors, vol. 1.
20. Though I have copied our historian, as the rest have copied him, in this date, I must desire the reader to take notice, that this very date is another of Sir T. More's errors; for in the public acts is a deed of Edward the Fifth, dated June 17th.

usurpation was not the goodness of his government, according to a common remark, that princes of doubtful titles make the best masters, as it is more necessary for them to conciliate the favour of the people: the natural corollary from which observation need not be drawn. Certain it is that in many parts of the kingdom, not poisoned by faction, he was much beloved; and even after his death the northern counties gave open testimony of their affection to his memory.

On the Sixth of July Richard was crowned, and soon after set out on a progress to York, on his way visiting Gloucester, the seat of his former duchy. And now it is that I must call up the attention of the reader, the capital and bloody scene of Richard's life being dated from this progress. The narrative teems with improbabilities and notorious falshoods, and is flatly contradicted by so many unquestionable facts, that if we have no other reason to believe the murder of Edward the Fifth and his brother, than the account transmitted to us, we shall very much doubt whether they ever were murdered at all. I will state the account, examine it, and produce evidence to confute it, and then the reader will form his own judgment on the matter of fact.

Richard before he left London, had taken no measures to accomplish the assassination; but on the road, "his mind misgave him,[21] that while his nephews lived, he should not possess the crown with security. Upon this reflection he dispatched one Richard Greene to Sir Robert Brakenbury, lieutenant of the Tower, with a letter and credence also, that the same Sir

21. Sir T. More.

53

Robert in any wise should put the two children to death. This John Greene did his errand to Brakenbury, kneeling before our Lady in the Tower, who plainly answered that he never would put them to death, to dye therefore." Green returned with this answer to the king who was then at Warwick, wherewith he took such displeasure and thought, that the same night he said unto a secret page of his, "Ah! whom' shall a man trust? They that I have brought up myself, they that I thought would have most surely served me, even those faile me. and at my commandment will do nothing for me." "Sir," quoth the page, "there lieth one in the palet chamber without, that I dare say will doe your grace pleasure; the thing were right hard that he would refuse;" meaning this by James Tirrel, whom, says Sir Thomas a few pages afterwards, as men say, he there made a knight. "The man," continues More, "had an high heart, and sore longed upwards, not rising yet so fast as he had hoped, being hindered and kept under by Sir Richard Ratcliffe and Sir William Catesby, who by secret drifts kept him out of all secret trust." To be short, Tirrel voluntarily accepted the commission, received warrant to authorize Brakenbury to deliver to him the keys of the Tower for one night; and having selected two other villains called Miles Forest and John Dighton, the two latter smothered the innocent princes in their beds, and then called Tirrel to be witness of the execution.

It is difficult to croud more improbabilities and lies together than are comprehended in this short narrative. Who can believe if Richard meditated the murder, that he took no care to sift Brakenbury before he left London? Who can believe that he would trust so atrocious a commission to a letter? And who can imagine, that on[22] Brakenbury's non-compliance Richard would have ordered him to cede the government of the Tower to Tirrel for one night only, the purpose of which had been so plainly pointed out by the preceding message? And had such weak steps been taken, could the murder itself have remained a problem? And yet Sir Thomas More himself is forced to confess at the outset of this very narration, "that the deaths and final fortunes of the two young princes have never-thelesse so far come in question, that some remained long in doubt, whether they were *in his days* destroyed[23] or no." Very memorable

22. It appears from the Foedera that Brakenbury was appointed Constable of the Tower July 7th;* that he surrendered his patent March 9th of the following year, and had one more ample granted to him. If it is supposed that Richard renewed this patent to Sir Robert Brakenbury, to prevent his disclosing what he knew of a murder, in which he had refused to be concerned, I then ask if it is probable that a man too virtuous or too cautious to embark in an assassination, and of whom the supposed tyrant stood in awe, would have laid down his life in that usurper's cause, as Sir Robert did, being killed on Richard's side at Bosworth, when many other of his adherents betrayed him?

23. This is confirmed by Lord Bacon: "Neither wanted there even at that time secret rumours and whisperings (which afterwards gathered strength, and turned to great trouble) that the two young sons of king Edward the Fourth, or one of them (which were said to be destroyed in the Tower) were not indeed murthered, but conveyed secretly away, and were yet living." Reign of Henry the Seventh, p. 4. again, p. 19. "And all this time it was still whispered every where that at least one of the children of Edward the Fourth was living."

words, and sufficient to balance More's own testimony with the most sanguine believers. He adds, "these doubts not only arose from the uncertainty men were in, whether Perkin Warbeck was the true duke of York, but for that also all things were so covertly demeaned, that there was nothing so plain and openly proved, but that yet men had it ever inwardly suspect." Sir Thomas goes on to affirm, "that he does not relate the story after every way that he had heard, but after that way that he had heard it by such men and such meanes, as he thought it hard but it should be true." This affirmation rests on the credibility of certain reporters, we do not know whom, but who we shall find were no credible reporters at all: for to proceed to the confutation. James Tirrel, a man in no secret trust with the king, and kept down by Catesby and Ratcliffe, is recommended as a proper person by a nameless page. In the first place Richard was crowned at York (after this transaction) September 8th.* Edward the Fourth had not been dead four months, and Richard in possession of any power not above two months, and those very bustling and active: Tirrel must have been impatient indeed, if the page had had time to observe his discontent at the superior confidence of Ratcliffe and Catesby. It happens unluckily too, that great part of the time Ratcliffe was absent, Sir Thomas More himself telling us that Sir Richard Ratcliffe had the custody of the prisoners at Pontefract, and presided at their execution there. But a much more unlucky circumstance is, that James Tirrel, said to be knighted for this horrid service, was not only a knight before, but a great or very considerable officer of the crown; and in that situation had walked at Richard's preceding coronation. Should I be told that Sir Thomas More did not mean to confine the ill offices done to Tirrel by Ratcliffe and Catesby solely to the time of Richard's protectorate and regal power, but being all three attached to him when duke of Gloucester, the other two might have lessened Tirrel's credit with the duke even in the preceding reign; then I answer, that Richard's appointing him master of the horse on his accession had removed those disgusts, and left the page no room to represent him as ready through ambition and despondency to lend his ministry to assassination. Nor indeed was the master of the horse likely to be sent to supersede the constable of the Tower for one night only. That very act was sufficient to point out what Richard desired to, and did, it seems, transact so covertly.

That Sir James Tirrel was and did walk as master of the horse at Richard's coronation cannot be contested.* A most curious, invaluable, and authentic monument has lately been discovered, the coronation-roll of Richard the Third. Two several deliveries of parcels of stuff are there expressly entered, as made to "Sir James Tirrel, knyght, maister of the hors of our sayd soverayn lorde the kynge." What now becomes of Sir Thomas More's informers, and of their narrative, which he thought hard but must be true?

I will go a step farther, and consider the evidence of this murder, as produced by Henry the Seventh some years afterwards, when, instead of lamenting it, it was necessary for his majesty to hope it had been true; at least to hope the people would think so. On the appearance of Perkin Warbeck, who gave himself out for the second of the brothers, who was believed so by

57

most people, and at least feared by the king to be so, he bestirred himself to prove that both the princes had been murdered by his predecessor. There had been but three actors, besides Richard who had commanded the execution, and was dead. These were Sir James Tirrel, Dighton, and Forrest; and these were all the persons whose depositions Henry pretended to produce; at least of two of them, for Forrest it seems had rotted piece-meal away; a kind of death unknown at present to the college. But there were some others, of whom no notice was taken; as the nameless page, Greene, one Black Will or Will Slaughter who guarded the princes, the friar who buried them, and Sir Robert Brakenbury, who could not be quite ignorant of what had happened: the latter was killed at Bosworth, and the friar was dead too. But why was no inquiry made after Greene and the page? Still this silence was not so impudent as the pretended confession of Dighton and Sir James Tirrel. The former certainly did avow the fact, and was suffered to go unpunished wherever he pleased – undoubtedly that he might spread the tale. And observe these remarkable words of lord Bacon, "John Dighton, who it seemeth *spake best for the king*, was forewith set at liberty." In truth, every step of this pretended discovery, as it stands in lord Bacon, warns us to give no heed to it. Dighton and Tirrel agreed both in a tale, *as the king gave out*. Their confession therefore was not publickly made, and as Sir James Tirrel too, was suffered to live;[24] but was shut up in the Tower, and put to

24.   It appears by Hall, that Sir James Tirrel had even enjoyed the favour of Henry; for Tirrel is named as

58

death afterwards for we know not what treason;* what can we believe, but that Dighton was some low mercenary wretch hired to assume the guilt of a crime he had not committed, and that Sir James Tirrel never did, never would confess what he had not done; and was therefore put out of the way on a fictitious imputation? It must be observed too, that no inquiry was made into the murder on the accession of Henry the Seventh, the natural time for it, when the passions of men were heated, and when the duke of Norfolk, lord Lovel, Catesby, Ratcliffe, and the real abettors or accomplices of Richard, were attainted and executed. No mention of such a murder was[25] made in the very act of parliament that attainted Richard himself, and which would have been the most heinous aggravation of his crimes. And no prosecution of the supposed assassins was even thought of till eleven years afterwards, on the appearance of Perkin Warbeck. Tirrel is not named in the act of

captain of Guisnes in a list of valiant officers that were sent by Henry, in his fifth year, on an expedition into Flanders. Does this look as if Tirrel was so much as suspected of the murder? And who can believe his pretended confession afterwards? Sir James was not executed till Henry's seventeenth year, on suspicion of treason, which suspicion arose on the flight of the earl of Suffolk. Vide Hall's Chronicle, fol. 18 & 55.

25. There is a heap of general accusations alledged to have been committed by Richard *against Henry*, in particular of his having *shed infant's blood*. Was this sufficient specification of the murder of a king? Is it not rather a base way of insinuating a slander, of which no proof could be given? Was not it consonant to all Henry's policy of involving every thing in obscure and general terms?

attainder to which I have had recourse; and such omissions cannot but induce us to surmise that Henry had never been certain of the deaths of the princes, nor ever interested himself to prove that both were dead, till he had great reason to believe that one of them was alive. Let me add, that if the confessions of Dighton and Tirrel were true, Sir Thomas More had no occasion to recur to the information of his unknown credible informers. If those confessions were not true, his informers were not creditable.

Having thus disproved the *account* of the murder, let us now examine whether we can be sure that the murder was committed.

Of all men it was most incumbent on cardinal Bourchier, archbishop of Canterbury, to ascertain the fact. To him had the queen entrusted her younger son, and the prelate had pledged himself for his security – unless every step of this history is involved in falshood. Yet what was the behaviour of the archbishop? He appears not to have made the least inquiry into the reports of the murder of both children; nay, not even after Richard's death: on the contrary, Bourchier was the very man who placed the crown on the head of the latter[26] and yet not one

26.　As cardinal Bourchier set the crown on Richard's head at Westminster, so did archbishop Rotherham at York.* These prelates either did not believe Richard had murdered his nephews, or were shamefully complaisant themselves. Yet their characters stand unimpeached in history. Could Richard be guilty, and the archbishops be blameless? Could both be ignorant what was become of the young princes, when both had negotiated with the queen dowager? As neither is accused of being the creature of Richard, it is probable that neither historian censures this conduct. Threats and fear could not have dictated this shameless negligence. Every body knows what was the authority of priests in that age; an archbishop was sacred, a cardinal inviolable. As Bourchier survived Richard, was it not incumbent on him to show, that the duke of York had been assassinated in spite of all his endeavours to save him? What can be argued from this inactivity of Bourchier, but that he did not believe the children were murdered?[27]

Richard's conduct in a parallel case is a strong presumption that this barbarity was falsely laid to his charge. Edward earl of Warwick, his nephew, and son of the duke of Clarence, was in his power too, and no indifferent rival, if king Edward's children were bastards. Clarence had been attainted; but so had almost every prince who had aspired to the crown after Richard the

of them believed he had taken off his nephews. In the Foedera there is a pardon passed to the archbishop, which at first made me suspect that he had taken some part in behalf of the royal children, as he is pardoned for all murders, treasons, concealments, misprisions, riots, routs, &c. but this pardon is not only dated Dec. 13, some months after he had crowned Richard; but, on looking farther, I find such pardons frequently granted to the most eminent of the clergy. In the next reign Walter, archbishop of Dublin, is pardoned all murders, rapes, treasons, felonies, misprisions, riots, routs, extortions, &c.

27. Lord Bacon tells us, that "on Simon's and Jude's even, the king (Henry the Seventh) dined with Thomas Bourchier, archbishop of Canterburie, and cardinal: and from Lambeth went by land over the bridge to the Tower." Has not this the appearance of some curiosity in the king on the subject of the princes, of whose fate he was uncertain?

Second. Richard duke of York, the father of Edward the Fourth and Richard the Third, was son of Richard earl of Cambridge, beheaded for treason; yet that duke of York held his father's attainder no bar to his succession. Yet how did Richard the Third treat his nephew and competitor, the young Warwick? John Rous, a zealous Lancastrian and contemporary shall inform us; and will at the same time tell us an important anecdote, maliciously suppressed or ignorantly omitted by all our historians. Richard actually proclaimed him heir to the crown after the death of his own son, and ordered him to be served next to himself and the queen, though he afterwards set him aside, and confined him to the castle of Sheriff-Hutton.[28] The very day after the battle of Bosworth, the usurper Richmond was so far from being led aside from attention to his interest by the glare of his new-acquired crown, that he sent for the earl of Warwick from Sheriff-Hutton and committed him to the Tower, from whence he never stirred more, falling a sacrifice to the inhuman jealousy of Henry, as his sister, the venerable countess of Salisbury, did afterwards to that of Henry the Eighth. Richard, on the contrary,

28. P. 218. Rous is the more to be credited for this fact, as he saw the earl of Warwick in company with Richard at Warwick the year before on the progress to York, which shows that the king treated his nephew with kindness, and did not confine him till the plots of his enemies thickening, Richard found it necessary to secure such as had any pretensions to the crown. This will account for his preferring the earl of Lincoln, who, being his sister's son, could have no prior claim before himself.

was very affectionate to his family: instances appear in his treatment of the earls of Warwick and Lincoln. The lady Ann Poole, sister of the latter, Richard had agreed to marry to the prince of Scotland.

The more generous behaviour of Richard to the same young prince (Warwick) ought to be applied to the case of Edward the Fifth, if no proof exists of the murder. But what suspicious words are those of Sir Thomas More, quoted above, and unobserved by all our historians: "*Some remained long in doubt,*" says he, "*whether they* (the children) *were in his* (Richard's) *days destroyed or no.*" If they were not destroyed *in his days*, in *whose* days were they murdered? Who will tell me that Henry the Seventh did not find, the eldest at least, prisoner in the Tower; and if he did, what was there in Henry's nature or character to prevent our surmizes going farther?

And here let me lament that two of the greatest men in our annals have prostituted their admirable pens, the one to blacken a great prince, the other to varnish a pitiful tyrant. I mean the two[29] chancellors, Sir Thomas More and lord Bacon. The most senseless stories of the mob are converted to history by the former; the latter is still more culpable; he has held up to the admiration of posterity, and what is worse, to the imitation of succeeding princes, a man

29.   It is unfortunate, that another great chancellor should have written a history with the same propensity to misrepresentation, I mean lord Clarendon. It is hoped no more chancellors will write our story, till they can divest themselves of that habit of their profession, apologizing for a bad cause.

whose nearest approach to wisdom was mean cunning; and has raised into a legislator, a sanguinary, sordid, and trembling usurper. Henry was a tyrannic husband, and ungrateful master; he cheated as well as oppressed his subjects,[30] bartered the honour of the nation for foreign gold, and cut off every branch of the royal family, to ensure possession to his no title. Had he had any title, he could claim it but from his mother, and her he set aside. But of all titles he preferred that of conquest, which, if allowable in a foreign prince, can never be valid in a native, but ought to make him the execration of his countrymen.

There is nothing strained in the supposition of Richard's sparing his nephew. At least it is certain *now*, that though he dispossessed, he undoubtedly treated him at first with indulgence, attention, and respect; and though the proof I am going to give must have mortified the friends of the dethroned young prince, yet it shewed great aversion to cruelty, and was an indication that Richard rather assumed the crown for a season, than as meaning to detain it always from his brother's posterity. It is well known that in the Saxon times nothing was more common in cases of minority than for the uncle to be preferred to the nephew; and though bastardizing his brother's children was, on this supposition, double dealing; yet I have no doubt but Richard went so far as to insinuate an

30. "He had no purpose to go through with any warre upon France; but the truth was, that hee did but traffique with that warre to make his returne in money." Ld Bacon's reign of Henry the Seventh, p. 99.

intention of restoring the crown when young
Edward should be of full age. I have three
strong proofs of this hypothesis. In the first
place Sir Thomas More reports that the duke of
Buckingham in his conversations with Morton,
after his defection from Richard, told the bishop
that the protector's first proposal had been to
take the crown, till Edward his nephew should
attain the age of twenty-four years. Morton was
certainly competent evidence of these dis-
courses, and therefore a credible one; and the
idea is confirmed by the two other proofs I
alluded to; the second of which was, that
Richard's son did *not* walk at his father's coronation. Sir Thomas More indeed says that Richard
created him prince of Wales on assuming the
crown; but this is one of Sir Thomas's misrepre-
sentations, and is contradicted by fact, for
Richard did not create his son prince of Wales
till he arrived at York;* a circumstance that
might lead the people to believe that in the
interval of the two coronations, the latter of
which was celebrated at York, September 8th,
the princes were murdered.

But though Richard's son did not walk at his
father's coronation, Edward the Fifth probably
did, and this is my third proof. I conceive all
the astonishment of my readers at this assertion,
and yet it is founded on strongly presumptive
evidence. In the[31] coronation roll itself is this

31. This singular curiosity was first mentioned to me
by the lord bishop of Carlisle. Mr. Astle lent me an
extract of it, with other useful assistances; and Mr.
Chamberlain of the great wardrobe obliged me
with the perusal of the original; favours which I
take this opportunity of gratefully acknowledging.

amazing entry; "To Lord Edward, son of late king Edward the Fourth, for his apparel and array, that is to say, a short gowne made of two yards and three quarters of crymsy clothe of gold, lyned with two yards $\frac{3}{4}$ of blac velvet, a long gowne made of vi yards D of crymsyn cloth of gold lynned with six yards of grene damask, a shorte gowne made of two yards $\frac{3}{4}$ of purpell velvett lyned with two yards $\frac{3}{4}$ of green damask, a doublett and a stomacher made of two yards of blac satyn, &c." besides two foot cloths, a bonet of purple velvet, nine horse harness, and nine saddle houses (housings) of blue velvet, gilt spurs, with many other rich articles, and magnificent apparel for his henchmen or pages.*

Let no body tell me that these robes, this magnificence, these trappings for a cavalcade, were for the use of a prisoner. Marvellous as the fact is, there can no longer be any doubt but the deposed young king walked, or it was intended should walk, at his uncle's coronation. This precious monument, a terrible reproach to Sir Thomas More and his copyists, who have been silent on so public an event, exists in the great wardrobe; and is in the highest preservation; it is written on vellom, and is bound with the coronation rolls of Henry the Seventh and Eighth. These are written on paper, and are in worse condition; but that of king Richard is uncommonly fair, accurate and ample. It is the account of Peter Courteys keeper of the great wardrobe, and dates from the day of king Edward the Fourth his death, to the feast of the purification in the February of the following year. Peter Courteys specifies what stuff he found in the wardrobe, what contracts he made for the ensuing coronation, and the deliveries in

66

consequence. The whole is couched in the most minute and regular manner, and is preferable to a thousand vague and interested histories. The concourse of nobility at that ceremony was extraordinarily great: there were present no fewer than three duchesses of Norfolk. Has this the air of a forced and precipitate election? Or does it not indicate a voluntary concurrence of the nobility? No mention being made in the roll of the young duke of York, no robes being ordered for him, it looks extremely as if he was not in Richard's custody; and strengthens the probability that will appear hereafter, of his having been conveyed away.

There is another article, rather curious than decisive of any point of history. One entry is thus; "To the lady Brygitt, oon of the daughters of K. Edward IIIIth, being seeke (sick) in the said wardrobe for to have for her use two long pillows of fustian stuffed with downe, and two pilow beres of Holland cloth." The only conjecture that can be formed from this passage is, that the lady Bridget, being lodged in the great wardrobe, was not then in sanctuary.*

Can it be doubted now but that Richard meant to have it thought that his assumption of the crown was only temporary? But when he proceeded to bastardize his nephew by act of parliament, then it became necessary to set him entirely aside: stronger proofs of the bastardy might have come out; and it is reasonable to infer this, for on the death of his own son, when Richard had no longer any reason of family to bar his brother Edward's children, instead of again calling them to the succession, as he at first projected or gave out he would, he settled the crown on the issue of his sister, Suffolk, declaring her eldest son the earl of Lincoln his successor.

That young prince was slain in the battle of Stoke against Henry the Seventh, and his younger brother the earl of Suffolk, who had fled to Flanders, was extorted from the archduke Philip, who by contrary winds had been driven into England. Henry took a solemn oath not to put him to death; but copying David rather than Solomon, he, on his death-bed, recommended it to his son Henry the Eighth to execute Suffolk; and Henry the Eighth was too pious not to obey so scriptural an injunction.

Strange as the fact was of Edward the Fifth walking at his successor's coronation, I have found an event exactly parallel which happened some years before. It is well known that the famous Joan of Naples was dethroned and murdered by the man she had chosen for her heir, Charles Durazzo. Ingratitude and cruelty were the characteristics of that wretch. He had been brought up and formed by his uncle Louis king of Hungary, who left only two daughters. Mary the eldest succeeded and was declared *king*; for that warlike nation, who regarded the sex of a word, more than of a person, would not suffer themselves to be governed by the term *queen*. Durazzo quitted Naples in pursuit of new ingratitude; dethroned *king Mary*, and obliged her to walk at his coronation; an insult she and her mother soon revenged by having him assassinated.

I do not doubt but the wickedness of Durazzo will be thought a proper parallel to Richard's. But parallels prove nothing: and a man must be a very poor reasoner who thinks he has an advantage over me, because I dare produce a circumstance that resembles my subject in the case to which it is applied, and leaves my argument just as strong as it was before in every other point.

They who the most firmly believe the murder of the two princes, and from what I have said it is plain that they believe it more strongly than the age did in which it was pretended to be committed; urge the disappearance[32] of the princes as a proof of the murder, but that argument vanishes entirely, at least with regard to one of them, if Perkin Warbeck was the true duke of York, as I shall show that it is greatly probable he was.

With regard to the elder, his disappearance is no kind of proof that he was murdered: he might die in the Tower. The queen pleaded to the archbishop of York that both princes were weak and unhealthy. I have insinuated that it is not impossible but Henry the Seventh might find him alive in the Tower. I mention that as a bare possibility – but we may be very sure that if he did find Edward alive there, he would not have notified his existence, to acquit Richard and hazard his own crown. The circumstances of the murder were evidently false, and invented by Henry to discredit Perkin; and the time of the murder is absolutely a fiction, for it appears by the roll of parliament, which bastardized

32. Polidore Vergil says, "In vulgus fama valuit filios Edwardi Regis aliquo terrarum partem migrasse, atque ita superstites esse." And the prior of Croyland, not his continuator,* whom I shall quote in the next note but one, and who was still better informed, "Vulgatum est regis Edwardi pueros concessisse in fata, sed quo genere interitus ignoratur"

69

Edward the Fifth, that he was then[33] alive, which was seven months after the time assigned

33. Buck asserts this from the parliament roll. The annotator in Kennett's collection says, "this author would have done much towards the credit he drives at in his history, to have specified the place of the roll and the words thereof, whence such arguments might be gathered; for," adds he, "all histories relate the murders to be committed before this time." I have shown that *all histories* are reduced to one history, Sir Thomas More's; for the rest copy him verbatim; and I have shown that his account is false and improbable. As the roll itself is now printed, in the parliamentary history, vol. 2.* I will point out the words that imply Edward the Fifth being alive when the act was passed. "Also it appeareth that *all* the issue of the said king Edward *be* bastards and unable to inherit or claim any thing by inheritance, by the law and custom of England." Had Edward the Fifth been dead, would not the act indubitably have run thus, *were and be bastards*. No, says the act, *all* the issue *are* bastards. Who were rendered uncapable to inherit but Edward the Fifth, his brother and sisters? Would not the act have specified the daughters of Edward the Fourth, if the sons had been dead? It was to bastardize the brothers, that the act was calculated and passed; and as the words *all the issue* comprehend males and females, it is clear that both were intended to be bastardized. I must however, impartially observe that Philip de Comines says, Richard having murdered his nephews, degraded their two sisters in full parliament. I will not dwell on his mistake of mentioning *two* sisters instead of five; but it must be remarked, that neither brothers nor sisters being specified in the act, but under the general term of king Edward's issue, it would naturally strike those who were uncertain what was become of the sons, that this act was levelled against the daughters. And as Comines did not write till some years after the event, he could not well help falling into that mistake. For

70

by More for his murder. If Richard spared him seven months, what could suggest a reason for his murder afterwards? To take him off then was strengthening the plan of the earl of Richmond, who aimed at the crown by marrying Elizabeth, eldest daughter of Edward the Fourth. As the house of York never rose again, as the reverse of Richard's fortune deprived him of any friend, and as no contemporaries but Fabian and the author of the Chronicle have written a word on that period, and they, too slightly to inform us, it is impossible to know whether Richard ever took any steps to refute the calumny. But we do know that Fabian only mentions the deaths of the *princes* as *reports*, which is proof that Richard never declared their deaths or the death of either, as he would probably have done if he had removed them for his own security. The confessions of Sir Thomas More and lord Bacon that many doubted of the murder, amount to a violent presumption that they were not murdered: and to a proof that their deaths were never declared. No man has ever doubted that Edward the Second, Richard the Second, and Henry the Sixth perished at the times that were given out. Nor Henry the Fourth, nor Edward the Fourth thought it would much help their titles to leave it doubtful whether their competitors existed or not. Observe too, that the

my own part I know not how to believe that Richard would have passed that act, if he had murdered the two princes. It was recalling a shocking crime, and to little purpose; for as no woman had at that time ever sat on the English throne in her own right, Richard had little reason to apprehend the claim of his neices.

chronicle of Croyland, after relating Richard's second coronation at York, says, it was advised by some in the sanctuary at Westminster to convey abroad some of king Edward's daughters, "ut si quid dictis masculis humanitus in Turri contingerat, nihilominus per salvandas personas filiarum, regnum aliquando ad veros rediret haeredes." He says not a word of the princes being murdered, only urges the fears of their friends that it might happen. This was a living witness, very bitter against Richard, who still never accuses him of destroying his nephews, and who speaks of them as living, after the time in which Sir Thomas More, who was not then five years old, declares they were dead. Thus the parliament roll and the chronicle agree, and both contradict More. "Interim & dum haec agerentur (the coronation at York) remanserunt duo predicti Edwardi regis filii sub certâ deputatâ custodiâ infra Turrim Londoniarum." These are the express words of the Chronicle, p. 567.

As Richard gained the crown by the illegitimacy of his nephews, his causing them to be murdered, would not only have shown that he did not trust to that plea, but would have transferred their claim to their sisters. And I must not be told that his intended marriage with his neice is an answer to my argument; for were that imputation true, which is very problematic, it had nothing to do with the murder of her brothers. And here the comparison and irrefragability of dates puts this matter out of all doubt. It was not till the very close of his reign that Richard is even supposed to have thought of marrying his neice. The deaths of his nephews are dated in July or August 1483. His own son did not die till April 1484, nor his queen till March 1485. He certainly therefore did not mean to strengthen his title by marrying his neice to the disinherison of his own son; and having on the loss of that son, declared his nephew the earl of Lincoln his successor, it is plain that he still trusted to the illegitimacy of his brother's children: and in no case possibly to be put, can it be thought that he wished to give strength to the claim of the princess Elizabeth.

Let us now examine the accusation of his intending to marry that neice: one of the consequences of which intention is a vague suspicion of poisoning his wife. Buck says that the queen was in a languishing condition, and that the physicians declared she could not hold out till April; and he affirms having seen in the earl of Arundel's library a letter written in passionate strains of love for her uncle by Elizabeth to the duke of Norfolk, in which she expressed doubts that the month of April would never arrive.* What is there in this account that looks like poison? Does it not prove that Richard would *not* hasten the death of his queen? The tales of poisoning for a time certain are now exploded; nor is it in nature to believe that the princess could be impatient to marry him, if she knew or thought he had murdered her brothers. Historians tell us that the queen took much to heart the death of her son, and never got over it. Had Richard been eager to wed his neice, and had his character been as impetuously wicked as it is represented, he would not have let the forward princess wait for the slow decay of her rival; nor did he think of it till nine months after the death of his son; which shows it was only to prevent Richmond's marrying her. His declaring his nephew his successor, implies at the same time no thought of getting rid of his queen, though he did not expect more issue from her: and little as Buck's authority is regarded, a cotemporary writer confirms the probability of this story. The Chronicle of Croyland says, that at[34] the Christmas festival, men were scandalized at seeing the queen and the lady Elizabeth dressed in robes similar and equally royal. I should suppose that Richard learning the projected marriage of Elizabeth and the earl of Richmond, amused the young princess with the hopes of making her his queen; and that Richard feared that alliance, is plain from his sending her to the castle of Sheriff-Hutton on the landing of Richmond.

The behaviour of the queen dowager must

34. "Per haec festa natalia choreis aut tripudiis, variisque mutatoriis vestium Annae reginae atque dominae Elizabeth, primogenitae defuncti regis, eisdem colore & forma distributis nimis intentum est: dictumque a multis est, ipsum regem aut expectatâ morte reginae aut per divortium, matrimonio cum dictâ Elizabeth contrahendo mentem omnibus modis applicare," p. 572. If Richard projected this match at Christmas, he was not likely to let these intentions be perceived so early, nor to wait till March, if he did not know that the queen was incurably ill. The Chroncile says, she died of a languishing distemper. Did that look like poison? It is scarce necessary to say that a dispensation from the pope was in that age held so clear a solution of all obstacles to the marriage of near relations, and was so easily to be obtained or purchased by a great prince, that Richard would not have been thought by his cotemporaries to have incurred any guilt, even if he had proposed to wed his neice, which however is far from being clear to have been his intention.

also be noticed. She was stripped by her son-in-law Henry of all her possessions, and confined to a monastery, for delivering up her daughters to Richard. Historians too are lavish in their censures on her for consenting to bestow her daughter on the murderer of her sons and brother. But if the murder of her sons is, as we have seen, most uncertain, this solemn charge falls to the ground: and for the deaths of her brother and lord Richard Grey, one of her elder sons, it has already appeared that she imputed them to Hastings. It is much more likely that Richard convinced her he had not murdered her sons, than that she delivered up her daughters to him believing it. The rigour exercised on her by Henry the Seventh on her countenancing Lambert Simnel, evidently set up to try the temper of the nation in favour of some prince of the house of York, is a violent presumption that the queen dowager believed her second son living: and notwithstanding all the endeavours of Henry to discredit Perkin Warbeck, it will remain highly probable that many more who ought to know the truth, believed so likewise; and that fact I shall examine next.

It was in the second year of Henry the Seventh that Lambert Simnel appeared. This youth first personated Richard duke of York, then Edward earl of Warwick; and was undoubtedly an impostor. Lord Bacon owns that it was whispered every-where, that *at least one* of the children of Edward the Fourth was living. Such whispers prove two things; one, that the murder was very uncertain: the second, that it would have been very dangerous to disprove the murder; Henry being at least as much interested as Richard had been to have the children dead.

Richard had set them aside as bastards, and thence had a title to the crown; but Henry was himself the issue of a bastard line, and had no title at all. Faction had set him on the throne, and his match with the supposed heiress of York induced the nation to wink at the defect in his own blood. The children of Clarence and of the duchess of Suffolk were living; so was the young duke of Buckingham, legitimately sprung from the youngest son of Edward the Third; whereas Henry came of the spurious stock of John of Gaunt. Lambert Simnel appeared before Henry had had time to disgust the nation, as he did afterwards, by his tyranny, cruelty, and exactions. But what was most remarkable, the queen dowager tampered in this plot. Is it to be believed, that mere turbulence and a restless spirit could in a year's time influence that woman to throw the nation again into a civil war, and attempt to dethrone her own daughter? And in favour of whom? Of the issue of Clarence, whom she had contributed to have put to death, or in favour of an impostor? There is not common sense in the supposition. No; she certainly knew or believed that Richard, her second son, had escaped and was living, and was glad to overturn the usurper without risking her child. The plot failed, and the queen dowager was shut up, where she remained till her death, "in prison,[35] poverty, and solitude." The king trumped up a silly accusation of her having delivered her daughters out of sanctuary to king Richard, "which proceeding," says the noble historian, "being even at that time taxed for rigorous and undue, makes it very probable

35. Lord Bacon.

there was some greater matter against her, which the king, upon reason of policie, and to avoid envy, would not publish." How truth sometimes escapes from the most courtly pens! What interpretation can be put on these words, but that the king found the queen dowager was privy to the escape at least or existence of her second son, and secured her, lest she should bear testimony to the truth, and foment insurrections in his favour? Lord Bacon adds, "It is likewise no small argument that *there was some secret in it*; for that the priest Simon himself (who set Lambert to work) after he was taken, was never brought to execution; no, not so much as to publicke triall, but was only shut up close in a dungeon. Adde to this, that after the earl of Lincoln (a principal person of the house of York) was slaine in Stokefield, the king opened himself to some of his councell, that he was sorie for the earl's death, because by him (he said) he might have known the bottom of his danger."

The earl of Lincoln had been declared heir to the crown by Richard, and therefore certainly did not mean to advance Simnel, an impostor, to it. It will be insinuated, and lord Bacon attributes that motive to him, that the earl of Lincoln hoped to open a way to the crown for himself. It might be so; still that will not account for Henry's wish, that the earl had been saved. On the contrary, one dangerous competitor was removed by his death; and therefore when Henry wanted to have learned *the bottom of his danger*, it is plain he referred to Richard duke of York, of whose fate he was still in doubt.[36]

36. The earl of Lincoln assuredly did not mean to blacken his uncle Richard by whom he had been

He certainly was; why else was it thought dangerous to visit or see the queen dowager after her imprisonment, as lord Bacon owns it was? "For that act," continues he, "the king sustained great obloquie; which nevertheless (besides the reason of state) was somewhat sweetened to him by a great confiscation." Excellent prince! This is the man in whose favour Richard the Third is represented as a monster!

"For Lambert, the king would not take his life," continues Henry's biographer, "both out of magnanimitie" (a most proper picture of so mean a mind!) "and likewise out of wisdom, thinking that if he suffered death he would be forgotten too soon; but being kept alive, he would be a continual spectacle, and a kind of remedy against the *like inchantments of people* in time to come." What! do lawful princes live in dread of a possibility of phantoms![37] Oh! no; but Henry knew what he had to fear; and he hoped by keeping up the memory of Simnel's

declared heir to the crown. One should therefore be glad to know what account he gave of the escape of the young duke of York. Is it probable that the earl of Lincoln gave out, that the elder had been murdered? It is more reasonable to suppose, that the earl asserted that the child had been conveyed away by means of the queen dowager or some other friend; and before I conclude this examination, that I think will appear most probably to have been the case.

37. Henry had so great a distrust of his right to the crown, that in his second year he obtained a bull from pope Innocent to qualify the privileges of sanctuaries, in which was this remarkable clause, "That if any took sanctuarie for case of treason, the king might appoint him keepers to look to him in sanctuarie." Lord Bacon, p. 39.

imposture, to discredit the true duke of York, as another puppet, when ever he should really appear.

That appearance did not happen till some years afterwards, and in Henry's eleventh year. Lord Bacon has taken infinite pains to prove a second imposture; and yet owns, "that the king's manner of shewing things by pieces and by darke lights, hath so muffled it, that it hath left it almost a mysterie to this day." What has he left a mystery? and what did he try to muffle? Not the imposture, but the truth. Had so politic a man any interest to leave the matter doubtful? Did he try to leave it so? On the contrary, his diligence to detect the imposture was prodigious. Did he publish his narrative to obscure or elucidate the transaction? Was it his manner to muffle any point that he could clear up, especially when it behoved him to have it cleared? When Lambert Simnel first personated the earl of Warwick, did not Henry exhibit that poor prince on a Sunday throughout all the principal streets of London? Was he not con-ducted to Paul's cross, and openly examined by the nobility? "which did in effect marre the pageant in Ireland." Was not Lambert himself taken into Henry's service, and kept in his court for the same purpose? In short, what did Henry ever muffle and disguise but the truth? and why was his whole conduct so different in the cases of Lambert and Perkin, if their cases were not totally different? No doubt remains on the former; the gross falshoods and contradictions in which Henry's account of the latter is involved, make it evident that he himself could never detect the imposture of the latter, if it was one. Dates, which every historian has neglected, again come to our aid, and cannot be controverted.

Richard duke of York was born in 1474.* Perkin Warbeck was not heard of before 1495, when duke Richard would have been Twenty-one. Margaret of York, duchess dowager of Burgundy, and sister of Edward the Fourth, is said by lord Bacon to have been the Juno who persecuted the pious Aeneas, Henry, and set up this phantom against him. She it was, say the historians, and says Lord Bacon, p. 115, "who informed Perkin of all the circumstances and particulars that concerned the person of Richard duke of York, which he was to act, describing unto him the personages, lineaments, and features of the king and queen, his pretended parents, and of his brother and sisters, and divers others that were nearest him in his childhood; together with all passages, some secret, some common, that were fit for a child's memory, until the death of king Edward. Then she added the particulars of the time, from the king's death, until he and his brother were committed to the Tower, as well during the time he was abroad, as while he was in sanctuary. As for the times while he was in the Tower, and the manner of his brother's death, and his own escape, she knew they were things that verie few could controle: and therefore she taught him only to tell a smooth and likely tale of those matters, warning him not to vary from it." Indeed! Margaret must in truth have been a Juno, a divine power, if she could give all these instructions to purpose. This passage is so very important, the whole story depends so much upon it, that if I can show the utter impossibility of its being true, Perkin will remain the true duke of York for any thing we can prove to the contrary; and for Henry, Sir Thomas More, lord Bacon, and their copyists, it will be impossible to give any longer credit to their narratives.

I have said that duke Richard was born in 1474. Unfortunately his aunt Margaret was married out of England in 1467, seven years before he was born, and never returned thither. Was not she singularly capable of describing to Perkin, her nephew, whom she had never seen? How well informed was she of the times of his childhood, and of all passages relating to his brother and sisters! Oh! but she had English refugees about her. She must have had many, and those of most intimate connection with the court, if she and they together could compose a tolerable story for Perkin, that was to take in the most minute passages of so many years.[38]

38. It would have required half the court of Edward the Fourth to frame a consistent legend. Let us state this in a manner that must strike our apprehension. The late princess royal was married out of England, before any of the children of the late prince of Wales were born. She lived no farther than the Hague; and yet who thinks that she could have instructed a Dutch lad in so many passages of the courts of her father and brother, that he would not have been detected in an hour's time. Twenty-seven years at least had elapsed since Margaret had been in the court of England. The marquis of Dorset, the earl of Richmond himself, and most of the fugitives had taken refuge in Bretagne, not with Margaret; and yet was she so informed of every trifling story, even those of the nursery, that she was able to pose Henry himself, and reduce him to invent a tale that had not a shadow of probability in it. Why did he not convict Perkin out of his own mouth? Was it ever pretended that Perkin failed in his part? That was the surest and

Who informed Margaret, that she might inform Perkin, of what passed in sanctuary? Ay; and who told her what passed in the Tower? Let the warmest asserter of the imposture answer that question, and I will give up all I have said in this work; yes, all. Forest was dead, and the supposed priest; Sir James Tirrel, and Dighton, were in Henry's hands. Had they trumpeted about the story of their own guilt and infamy, till Henry, *after* Perkin's appearance, found it necessary to publish it? Sir James Tirrel and Dighton had certainly never gone to the court of Burgundy to make a merit with Margaret of having murdered her nephews. How came she to know accurately and authentically a tale which no mortal else knew? Did Perkin or did he not correspond in his narrative with Tirrel and Dighton? If he did, how was it possible for him to know it? If he did not, is it morally credible that Henry would not have made those variations public? If Edward the Fifth was murdered, and the duke of York saved, Perkin could know it but by being the latter. If he did not know it, what was so obvious as his detection? We must allow Perkin to be the true duke of York, or give up the whole story of Tirrel and Dighton. When Henry had Perkin, Tirrel, and Dighton, in his power, he had nothing to do but to confront them, and the

best proof of his being an impostor. Could not the whole court, the whole kingdom of England, so cross-examine this Flemish youth, as to catch him in one lie? No; lord Bacon's Juno had inspired him with full knowledge of all that had passed in the last twenty years. If Margaret was Juno, he who shall answer these questions satisfactorily, "erit mihi magnus Apollo."

imposture was detected. It would not have been sufficient that Margaret had enjoined him *to tell a smooth and likely tale of those matters*. A man does not tell a likely tale, nor was a *likely* tale enough, of matters of which he is totally ignorant.

Still farther: why was Perkin never confronted with the queen dowager, with Henry's own queen, and with the princesses, her sisters? Why were they never asked, Is this your son? Is this your brother? Was Henry afraid to trust to their natural emotions? Yet "he himself," says lord Bacon, p. 186, "saw him sometimes out of a window, or in passage." This implies that the queens and princesses never did see him; and yet they surely were the persons who could best detect the counterfeit, if he had been one. Had the young man made a *voluntary*, coherent, and credible confession, no other evidence of his imposture would be wanted; but failing that, we cannot help asking, Why the obvious means of detection were not employed? Those means having been omitted, our suspicions remain in full force.

Henry, who thus neglected every means of confounding the impostor, took every step he would have done, if convinced that Perkin was the true duke of York. His utmost industry was exerted in sifting to the bottom of the plot, in learning who was engaged in the conspiracy, and in detaching the chief supporters. It is said, though not affirmatively, that to procure confidence to his spies, he caused them to be solemnly cursed at Paul's cross. Certain it is, that, by their information, he came to the knowledge, not of the imposture, but of what rather tended to prove that Perkin was a genuine Plantagenet: I mean, such a list of great men actually in his court and in trust about his person, that no wonder he was seriously alarmed. Sir Robert Clifford,[39] who had fled to Margaret, wrote to England, that he was positive that the claimant was the very identical duke of York, son of Edward the Fourth, whom he had so often seen, and was perfectly acquainted with. This man, Clifford, was bribed back to Henry's service; and what was the consequence? He accused Sir William Stanley, lord Chamberlain, the very man who had set the crown on Henry's head in Bosworth field, and own brother to the earl of Derby, the then actual husband of Henry's mother, of being in the conspiracy? This was indeed essential to Henry to know; but what did it proclaim to the nation? What could stagger the allegiance of such trust and such connexions, but the firm persuasion that Perkin was the true duke of York? A spirit of faction and disgust has even in later times hurried men into treasonable combinations; but however Sir William Stanley might be dissatisfied, as not thinking himself adequately rewarded, yet is it credible that he should risk such favour, such riches, as lord Bacon allows he possessed, on the wild bottom of a Flemish counterfeit? The lord Fitzwalter and other great men suffered in the fame cause; and which is remarkable, the first was executed at Calais — another presumption that Henry would not venture to have his evidence made public. And the strongest presumption of all is, that not one of the sufferers is pretended to have recanted; they all died then in the persuasion

39. A gentleman of fame and family, says lord Bacon.

that they had engaged in a righteous cause. When peers, knights of the garter, privy councellors, suffer death, from conviction of a matter of which they were proper judges (for which of them but must know their late master's son?) it would be rash indeed in us to affirm that they laid down their lives for an imposture, and died with a lie in their mouths.

What can be said against king James of Scotland, who bestowed a lady of his own blood in marriage on Perkin?* At war with Henry, James would naturally support his rival, whether genuine or suppositious. He and Charles the Eighth both gave him aid and both gave him up, as the wind of their interest shifted about. Recent instances of such conduct have been seen; but what prince has gone so far as to stake his belief in a doubtful cause, by sacrificing a princess of his own blood in confirmation of it?

But it is needless to multiply presumptions. Henry's conduct and the narrative[40] he published, are sufficient to stagger every impartial reader.* Lord Bacon confesses *the king did himself no good* by the publication of that narrative, and that mankind was astonished to find no mention in it of the duchess Margaret's machinations. But how could lord Bacon stop there? Why did he not conjecture that there was no proof of that tale? What interest had Henry to manage a widow of Burgundy? He had applied to the archduke Philip to banish Perkin: Philip replied, he had no power over the lands of the

40.   To what degree arbitrary power dares to trifle with the common sense of mankind has been seen in Portuguese and Russian manifestos.

duchess's dowry. It is therefore most credible that the duchess had supported Perkin, on the persuasion he was her nephew; and Henry not being able to prove the reports he had spread of her having trained up an impostor, chose to drop all mention of Margaret, because nothing was so natural as her supporting the heir of her house. On the contrary, in Perkin's confession, as it was called, and which though preserved by Grafton, was suppressed by lord Bacon, not only as repugnant to his lordship's account, but to common sense, Perkin affirms, that "having sailed to Lisbon in a ship with the lady Brampton, who, lord Bacon says, was sent by Margaret to conduct him thither, and from thence having resorted to Ireland, it was at Cork that they of the town first threaped upon him that he was son of the duke of Clarence; and others afterwards, that he was the duke of York." But the contradictions both in lord Bacon's account, and in Henry's narrative, are irreconcileable and insurmountable: the former solves the likeness,[41] which is allowing the likeness, of Perkin to Edward the Fourth, by supposing that the king had an intrigue with his mother; of which he gives this silly relation: that Perkin Warbeck, whose surname it seems was Peter Osbeck, was son of a Flemish converted Jew (of which Hebrew extraction Perkin says not a[42]

41. As this solution of the likeness is not authorized by the youth's supposed narrative, the likeness remains uncontrovertible, and consequently another argument for his being king Edward's son.
42. On the contrary, Perkins calls his grandfather Diryck Osbeck; Diryck every body knows is Theodoric, and Theodoric is certainly no Jewish

86

word in his confession) who with his wife Katherine de Faro come to London on business; and she producing a son, king Edward, in consideration of the conversion, or intrigue, stood godfather to the child and gave him the name of *Peter*. Can one help laughing at being told that a king called *Edward* gave the name of *Peter* to his godson? But of this transfretation and christening Perkin, in his supposed confession, says not a word, nor pretends to have ever set foot in England, till he landed there in pursuit of the crown; and yet an English birth and some stay, though in his very childhood, was a better way of accounting for the purity of his accent, then either of the preposterous tales produced by lord Bacon or by Henry. The former says, that Perkin, roving up and down between Antwerp and Tournay and other towns, and living much in English company, had the English tongue perfect. Henry was so afraid of not ascertaining a good foundation of Perkin's English accent, that he makes him learn the language twice over.[43] "Being sent with a merchant of Turney, called Berlo, to the mart of Antwerp, the said Berlo set me," says Perkin, "to borde in a skinner's house, that dwelled beside the house of the English nation. And after this the sayd Berlo set me with a merchant of Middelborough to service for[44] *to*

appelation. Perkin too mentions several of his relations and their employments at Tournay, without any hint of a Hebrew connection.
43. Grafton's Chronicle, p. 930.
44. I take this to mean the English language, for these reasons; he had just before named the English nation, and the name of his master was John

learne the language, with whom I dwelled from Christmas to Easter, and then I went into Portyngale." One does not learn any language

Strewe, which seems to be an English appellation: but there is a stronger reason for believing it means the English language, which is, that a Flemish lad is not set to learn his own language; though even this absurdity is advanced in this same pretended confession, Perkin affirming that his mother, after he had dwelled some time in Tournay, sent him to Antwerp to learn Flemish. If I am told by a very improbable supposition, that French was his native language at Tournay, that he learned Flemish at Antwerp, and Dutch at Middleburg, I will desire the objector to cast his eye on the map, and consider the small distance between Tournay, Middleburg, and Antwerp, and to reflect that the present United Provinces were not then divided from the rest of Flanders; and then to decide whether the dialects spoken at Tournay, Antwerp, and Middleburg were so different in that age, that it was necessary to be set to learn them all separately. If this cannot be answered satisfactorily, it will remain, that Perkin learned Flemish or English twice over. I am indifferent which, for still there will remain a contradiction in the confession. And if English is not meant in the passage above, it will only produce a greater difficulty, which is, that Perkin at the age of twenty learned to speak English in Ireland with so good an accent, that all England could not discover the cheat. I must be answered too, why lord Bacon rejects the youth's own confession and subtitutes another in its place, which makes Perkin born in England, though in his pretended confession Perkin affirms the contrary. Lord Bacon too confirms my interpretation of the passage in question, by saying that Perkin roved up and down between Antwerp and other towns in Flanders, living much in English company, and having the English tongue perfect, p. 115.

very perfectly and with a good, nay, undistinguishable accent, between Christmas and Easter;
but here let us pause. If this account was true,
the other relating to the duchess Margaret was
false; and then how came Perkin by so accurate a
knowledge of the English court, that he did not
faulter, nor could be detected in his tale? If the
confession was *not* true, it remains that it was
trumped up by Henry, and then Perkin must be
allowed the true duke of York.

But the gross contradiction of all follows: "It
was in Ireland," says Perkin, in this very
narrative and confession, "that against my will
they made me to learne English, and taught me
what I should do and say." Amazing! what
forced him to learn English, after, as he says
himself in the very same page, he had learnt it
at Antwerp! What an impudence was there in
royal power to dare to obtrude such stuff on the
world! Yet this confession, as it is called, was
the poor young man forced to read at his
execution — no doubt in dread of worse torture.
Mr. Hume, though he questions it, owns that it
was believed by torture to have been drawn from
him. What matters how it was obtained, or
whether ever obtained; it could not be true: and
as Henry could put together no more plausible
account, commiseration will shed a tear over a
hapless youth, sacrificed to the fury and jealousy
of an usurper, and in all probability the victim
of a tyrant, who has made the world believe that
the duke of York, executed by his own orders,
had been previously murdered by his
predecessor. [45]*

45.   Mr. Hume, to whose doubts all respect is due,
       tells me he thinks no mention being made of

I have thus, I flatter myself, from the discovery of new authorities, from the comparison of dates, from fair consequences and arguments, and without straining or wresting probability, proved all I pretended to prove; not an hypothesis of Richard's universal innocence, but this assertion with which I set out, that we have no reasons, no authority for believing by far the greater part of the crimes charged on him. I have convicted historians of partiality, absurdities, contradictions, and falshoods; and though I have destroyed their credit, I have ventured to establish no peremptory conclusion of my own. What did really happen in so dark a period, it would be rash to affirm. The coronation and parliament rolls have ascertained a few facts, either totally unknown, or misrepresented by historians. Time may bring other monuments to light:[46] but one thing is sure, that should any

Perkin's title in the Cornish rebellion under the lord Audeley, is a strong presumption that the nation was not persuaded of his being the true duke of York. This argument, which at most is negative, seems to me to lose its weight, when it is remembered, that this was an insurrection occasioned by a poll-tax: that the rage of the people was directed against archbishop Morton and Sir Reginald Bray, the supposed authors of the grievance. An insurrection against a tax in a southern county, in which no mention is made of a pretender to the crown, is surely not so forcible a presumption against him, as the persuasion of the northern counties that he was the true heir, is an argument in his favour. Much less can it avail against such powerful evidence as I have shown exists to overturn all that Henry could produce against Perkin.

46.   If diligent search was to be made in the public offices and convents of the Flemish towns in which

man hereafter presume to repeat the same improbable tale on no better grounds that it has been hitherto urged, he must shut his eyes against conviction, and prefer ridiculous tradition to the scepticism due to most points of history, and to none more than to that in question.

I have little more to say, and only on what regards the person of Richard and the story of Jane Shore; but having run counter to a very valuable modern historian and friend of my own, I must both make some apology for him, and for myself for disagreeing with him. When Mr. Hume published his reigns of Edward the Fifth, Richard the Third, and Henry the Seventh, the coronation roll had not come to light. The stream of historians concurred to make him take this portion of our story for granted. Buck had been given up as an advancer of paradoxes, and nobody but Carte had dared to controvert the popular belief. Mr. Hume treats Carte's doubts as whimsical: I wonder, he did; he, who having so closely examined our history, had discovered how very fallible many of its authorities are. Mr. Hume himself had ventured to contest both the flattering picture drawn of Edward the First, and those ignominious portraits of Edward the Second and Richard the Second. He had discovered from the Foedera, that Edward the Fourth, while said universally to be prisoner to archbishop Nevil, was at full liberty and doing acts of royal power. Why was it whimsical in Carte to exercise the same spirit

the duchess Margaret resided, I should not despair of new lights being gained to that part of our history.

of criticism? Mr. Hume could not but know how much the characters of princes are liable to be flattered or misrepresented. It is of little importance to the world, to Mr. Hume, or to me, whether Richard's story is fairly told or not: and in this amicable discussion I have no fear of offending him by disagreeing with him. His abilities and sagacity do not rest on the shortest reign in our annals. I shall therefore attempt to give answers to the questions on which he pins the credibility due to the history of Richard.

The questions are these. 1. Had not the queen-mother and the other heads of the York party been fully assured of the death of both the young princes, would they have agreed to call over the earl of Richmond, the head of the Lancastrian party, and marry him to the princess Elizabeth? — I answer, that when the queen-mother could recall that consent, and send to her son the marquis Dorset to quit Richmond, assuring him of king Richard's favour to him and her house, it is impossible to say what so weak and ambitious a woman would not do. She wanted to have some one of her children on the throne, in order to recover her own power. She first engaged her daughter to Richmond and then to Richard. She might not know what was become of her sons; and yet that is no proof they were murdered. They were out of her power, whatever was become of them; and she was impatient to rule. If she was fully assured of their deaths, could Henry, after he came to the crown and had married her daughter, be uncertain of it? I have shown that both Sir Thomas More and lord Bacon own it remained uncertain, and that Henry's account could not be true. As to the heads of the

Yorkists;[47] how does it appear they concurred in the projected match? Indeed who were the heads of that party? Margaret duchess of Burgundy, Elizabeth duchess of Suffolk, and her children; did they ever concur in that match? Did not they to the end endeavour to defeat and overturn it? I hope Mr. Hume will not call bishop Morton, the duke of Buckingham, and Margaret countess of Richmond, chiefs of the Yorkists. 2. The story told constantly by Perkin of his escape is utterly incredible, that those who were sent to murder his brother, took pity on him and granted him his liberty. – Answer. We do not know but from Henry's narrative and the Lancastrian historians that Perkin gave this account[48] I am not authorized to believe he did,

47.   The excessive affection shown by the Northern counties, where the principal strength of the Yorkists lay, to Richard the Third while living, and to his memory when dead, implies two things; first, that the party did *not* give him up to Henry; secondly, that they did not believe he had murdered his nephews. Tyrants of that magnitude are not apt to be popular. Examine the list of the chiefs in Henry's army, as stated by the Chronicle of Croyland, p. 574. and they will be found Lancastrians, or very private gentlemen, and but one peer, the earl of Oxford, a noted Lancastrian.

48.   Grafton has preserved a ridiculous oration said to be made by Perkin to the king of Scotland, in which this silly tale is told. Nothing can be depended upon less than such orations, almost always forged by the writer, and unpardonable, if they pass the bounds of truth. Perkin, in the passage in question, uses these words: "And farther to the entent that my life might be in a suretie he (the murderer of my elder brother) appointed one to convey me into some straunge countrie, where, when I was furthest off, and had most neede of

because I find no authority for the murder of the
elder brother; and if there was, why is it utterly
incredible that the younger should have been
spared? 3. What became of him during the
course of seven years from his supposed death
till his appearance in 1491? – Answer. Does
uncertainty of where a man has been, prove his
non-identity when he appears again? When Mr.
Hume will answer half the questions in this
work, I will tell him where Perkin was during
those seven years. 4. Why was not the queen-
mother, the duchess of Burgundy, and the other
friends of the family, applied to, during that
time, for his support and education? – Answer.
Who knows that they were not applied to? The
probability is, that they were. The queen's
dabbling in the affair of Simnel indicates that
she knew her son was alive. And when the
duchess of Burgundy is accused of setting Perkin to work, it is amazing that she should be
quoted as knowing nothing about him. 5.
Though the duchess of Burgundy at last ack-

comfort, he forsooke me sodainly (I think he was so
appointed to do) and left me desolate alone without friend or knowledge of any reliefe or refuge,
&c." Would not one think one was reading the tale
of Valentine and Orson, or any legend of a
barbarous age, rather than the history of England,
when we are told of *strange countries* and such
indefinite ramblings, as would pass only in a
nursery? It remains not only a secret but a doubt,
whether the elder brother was murdered. If Perkin
was the younger, and knew certainly that his
brother was put to death, our doubt would vanish:
but can it vanish on no better authority than this
foolish oration? Did Grafton hear it pronounced?
Did king James bestow his kinswoman on Perkin,
on the strength of such a fable?

94

nowledged him for her nephew, she had lost all
pretence to authority by her former acknow-
ledgement and support of Lambert Simnel, an
avowed impostor. – Answer. Mr. Hume here
makes an unwary confession by distinguishing
between Lambert Simnel, an avowed impostor,
and Perkin, whose imposture was problematic.
But if he was a true prince, the duchess could
only forfeit credit for herself, not for him: nor
would her preparing the way for her nephew, by
first playing off and feeling the ground by a
counterfeit, be an imputation on her, but rather
a proof of her wisdom and tenderness. Impostors
are easily detected; as Simnel was. All Henry's
art and power could never verify the cheat of
Perkin; and if the latter was astonishingly
adroit, the king was ridiculously clumsy. 6.
Perkin himself confessed his imposture more
than once, and read his confession to the people,
and renewed his confession at the foot of the
gibbet on which he was executed. – Answer. I
have shown that this confession was such an
aukward forgery that lord Bacon did not dare to
quote or adhere to it, but invented a new story,
more specious, but equally inconsistent with
probability. 7. After Henry the Eighth's accession, the titles of the houses of York and
Lancaster were fully confounded, and there was
no longer any necessity for defending Henry the
Seventh and his title; yet all the historians of
that time, when the events were recent, some of
these historians, such as Sir Thomas More, of
the highest authority, agree in treating Perkin
as an impostor. – Answer. When Sir Thomas
More wrote, Henry the Seventh was still alive;*
that argument therefore falls entirely to the
ground: but there *was* great necessity, I will not

say to defend, but even to palliate the titles of both Henry the Seventh and Eighth. The former, all the world agrees now, had no title:[49] the latter had none from his father, and a very defective one from his mother. If she had any right, it could only be after her brothers; and it is not to be supposed that so jealous a tyrant as Henry the Eighth would suffer it to be said that his father and mother enjoyed the throne to the prejudice of that mother's surviving brother, in whose blood the father had imbrued his hands. The murder therefore was to be fixed on Richard the Third, who was to be supposed to have usurped the throne, by murdering, and not, as was really the case, by bastardizing his nephews. If they were illegitimate, so was their sister; and if she was, what title had she conveyed to her son Henry the Eighth? No wonder that both Henrys were jealous of the earl of Suffolk, whom one bequeathed to slaughter, and the other executed; for if the children of Edward the Fourth were spurious, and those of Clarence attainted, the right of the house of York was vested in the duchess of Suffolk and her descendants. The massacre of the children of

49. Henry was so reduced to make out any title to the crown, that he catched even at a quibble. In the act of attainder, passed after his accession, he calls himself nephew of Henry the Sixth. He was so, but it was by his father, who was not of the blood royal. Catharine of Valois, after bearing Henry the Sixth, married Owen Tudor, and had two sons, Edmund and Jasper, the former of which married Margaret, mother of Henry the Seventh, and so was he half nephew of Henry the Sixth. On one side he had no blood royal, on the other only bastard blood.

Clarence and the duchess of Suffolk show what Henry the Eighth thought of the titles both of his father and mother[50] But, says Mr. Hume, all the historians of that time agree in treating Perkin as an impostor. I have shown from their own mouths that they all doubted of it. The reader must judge between us. But Mr. Hume selects Sir Thomas More as the highest authority; I have proved that he was the lowest – but not in the case of Perkin, for Sir Thomas More's history does not go so low; yet happening to mention him, he says, the man, commonly called Perkin Warbeck, was, as well with the princes as the people, held to be the younger son of Edward the Fourth; and that the deaths of the young king Edward and of Richard his brother had come so far in question, as some are yet in doubt, *whether they were destroyed or no in the days of king* Richard. Sir Thomas adhered to the affirmative, relying as I have shown on very bad authorities. But what is a stronger argument ad hominem, I can prove that Mr. Hume did not think Sir Thomas More good authority; no, Mr. Hume was a fairer and more impartial judge: at the very time that he quotes Sir Thomas More, he tacitly rejects his authority; for Mr. Hume, agreeably to truth, specifies the lady Eleanor Butler as the person to whom king Edward was contracted, and not Elizabeth Lucy, as it stands in Sir Thomas More. An attempt to vindicate Richard will perhaps no longer be thought whimsical, when so very acute a reasoner as Mr

50.   Observe, that when lord Bacon wrote, there was great necessity to vindicate the title even of Henry the Seventh, for James the First claimed from the eldest daughter of Henry and Elizabeth.

Hume could find no better foundation than these seven queries on which to rest his condemnation.

With regard to the person of Richard, it appears to have been as much misrepresented as his actions. Philip de Comines, who was very free spoken even on his own masters, and therefore not likely to spare a foreigner, mentions the beauty of Edward the Fourth; but says nothing of the deformity of Richard, though he saw them together. This is merely negative. The old countess of Desmond, who had danced with Richard, declared he was the handsomest man in the room except his brother Edward, and was very well made.* But what shall we say to Dr. Shaw, who in his sermon appealed to the people, whether Richard was not the express image of his father's person, who was neither ugly nor deformed? Not all the protector's power could have kept the muscles of the mob in awe and prevented their laughing at so ridiculous an apostrophe, had Richard been a little, crooked, withered, hump-back'd monster, as later historians would have us believe – and very idly? Cannot a foul soul inhabit a fair body?

The truth I take to have been this. Richard, who was slender and not tall, had one shoulder a little higher than the other: a defect, by the magnifying glasses of party, by distance of time, and by the amplification of tradition, easily swelled to shocking deformity; for falshood itself generally pays so much respect to truth as to make it the basis of its superstructures.

I have two reasons for believing Richard was not well made about the shoulders. Among the drawings which I purchased at Vertue's sale was one of Richard and his queen, of which nothing is expressed but the out-lines. There is no intimation from whence the drawing was taken; but by a collateral direction for the colour of the robe, if not copied from a picture, it certainly was from some painted window; where existing I do not pretend to say: in this whole work I have not gone beyond my vouchers.* Richard's face is very comely, and corresponds singularly with the portrait of him in the preface to the Royal and Noble Authors. He has a sort of tippet of ermine doubled about his neck, which seems calculated to disguise some want of symmetry thereabouts. I have given two[51] of this drawing, which is on large folio paper, that it may lead to a discovery of the original, if not destroyed.

My other authority is John Rous, the antiquary of Warwickshire, who saw Richard at Warwick in the interval of his two coronations, and who describes him thus: "Parvae staturae erat, curtam habens faciem, inaequales humeros, dexter superior, sinisterque inferior." What feature in this portrait gives any idea of a monster? Or who can believe that an eye-witness, and so minute a painter, would have mentioned nothing but the inequality of shoulders, if Richard's form had been a compound of ugliness? Could a Yorkist have drawn a less disgusting representation? And yet Rous was a vehement Lancastrian; and the moment he ceased to

51.   In the prints, the single head is most exactly copied from the drawing, which is unfinished. In the double plate, the reduced likeness of the king could not be so perfectly preserved.

have truth before his eyes, gave into all the virulence and forgeries of his party, telling us in another place, "that Richard remained two years in his mother's womb, and came forth at last with teeth, and hair on his shoulders." I leave it to the learned in the profession to decide whether women can go two years with their burden, and produce a living infant; but that this long pregnancy did not prevent the duchess, his mother, from bearing afterwards, I can prove; and could we recover the register of the births of her children, I should not be surprized to find, that, as she was a very fruitful woman, there was not above a year between the birth of Richard and his preceding brother Thomas.[52] However, an ancient[53] bard, who wrote after Richard was born and during the life of his father, tells us,

Richard liveth yit, but the last of all
Was Ursula, to him whom God list call.

Be it as it will, this foolish tale, with the

---

52. The author I am going to quote, gives us the order in which the duchess Cecily's children were born, thus; Ann duchess of Exeter, Henry, Edward the Fourth, Edmund earl of Rutland, Elizabeth duchess of Suffolk, Margaret duchess of Burgundy, William, John, George duke of Clarence, Thomas, Richard the Third, and Ursula. Cox, in his History of Ireland, says, that Clarence was born in 1451. Buck computed Richard the Third to have fallen at the age of thirty-four or five; but, by Cox's account, he could not be more than thirty-two.* Still this makes it probable, that their mother bore them and their intervening brother Thomas as soon as she well could one after another.

53. See Vincent's Erros in Brooke's Heraldy, p. 623.*

circumstances of his being born with hair and teeth, was coined to intimate how careful Providence was, when it formed a tyrant, to give due warning of what was to be expected. And yet these portents were far from prognosticating a tyrant; for this plain reason, that all other tyrants have been born without these prognostics. Does it require more time to ripen a foetus, that is, to prove a destroyer, than it takes to form an Aristides? Are there outward and visible signs of a bloody nature? Who was handsomer than Alexander, Augustus, or Louis the Fourteenth? and yet who ever commanded the spilling of more human blood?

Having mentioned John Rous, it is necessary I should say something more of him, as he lived in Richard's time, and even wrote his reign; and yet I have omitted him in the list of contemporary writers. The truth is, he was pointed out to me after the preceding sheets were finished; and upon inspection I found him too despicable and lying an author, even amongst monkish authors, to venture to quote him, but for two facts; for the one of which as he was an eye-witness, and for the other, as it was of publick notoriety, he is competent authority.

The first is his description of the person of Richard; the second, relating to the young earl of Warwick, I have recorded in its place.

This John Rous, so early as in the reign of Edward the Fourth, had retired to the hermitage of Guy's Cliff, where he was a chantry priest, and where he spent the remaining part of his life in what he called studying and writing antiquities. Amongst other works, most of which are *not* unfortunately lost, he composed a history of the kings of England. It begins with the creation, and is compiled indiscriminately from the Bible and from monastic writers. Moses, he tells us, does not mention all the cities founded before the deluge, but Bernard de Breydenback, dean of Mayence, does. With the same taste he acquaints us, that, though the Book of Genesis says nothing of the matter, Giraldus Cambrensis writes, that Caphera or Cesara, Noah's niece, being apprehensive of the deluge, set out for Ireland, where, with three men and fifty women, she arrived safe with one ship, the rest perishing in the general destruction.

A history, so happily begun, never falls off: prophecies, omens, judgments, and religious foundations compose the bulk of the book. The lives and actions of our monarchs, and the great events of their reigns, seemed to the author to deserve little place in a history of England. The lives of Henry the Sixth and Edward the Fourth, though the author lived under both, take up but two pages in octavo, and that of Richard the Third, three. We may judge how qualified such an author was to clear up a period so obscure, or what secrets could come to his knowledge at Guy's Cliff: accordingly he retails all the vulgar reports of the times; as that Richard poisoned his wife, and put his nephews to death, though he owns few knew in what manner; but as he lays the scene of their deaths *before* Richard's assumption of the crown, it is plain he was the worst informed of all. To Richard he ascribes the death of Henry the Sixth; and adds, that many persons believed he executed the murder with his own hands: but he records another circumstance that alone must weaken all suspicion of Richard's guilt in that transaction. Richard not only caused the body to be removed from Chertsey, and solemnly interred at Windsor, but it was publickly exposed, and, if we will believe the monk, was found almost entire, and emitted a gracious perfume, though no care had been taken to embalm it. Is it credible that Richrd, if the murderer, would have exhibited this unnecessary mummery, only to revive the memory of his own guilt? Was it not rather intended to recall the cruelty of his brother Edward, whose children he had set aside, and whom by the comparison of this act of piety, he hoped to[54] depreciate in the eyes of the people? The very example had been pointed out to him by Henry the Fifth, who bestowed a pompous funeral on Richard the Second, murdered by order of his father.

Indeed the devotion of Rous to that Lancastrian saint, Henry the Sixth, seems chiefly to engross his attention, and yet it draws him into a contradiction; for having said that the murder of Henry the Sixth had made Richard detested by all nations who heard of it, he adds, two pages afterwards, that an embassy arrived at Warwick (while Richard kept his court there) from the[55] king of Spain, to propose a marriage

54. This is not a mere random conjecture, but corroborated by another instance of like address. He disforested a large circuit, which Edward had annexed to the forest of Whichwoode, to the great annoyance of the subject. This we are told by Rous himself, p. 316.

55. Drake says, that an embassador from the queen of Spain was present at Richard's coronation at York. Rous himself owns, that, amidst a great concourse of nobility that attended the king at York, was the duke of Albany, brother of the king of Scotland.* Richard therefore appears not to have been abhorred by either the courts of Spain or Scotland.

between their children. Of this embassy Rous is a proper witness: Guy's Cliff, I think, is but four miles from Warwick; and he is too circumstantial on what passed there not to have been on the spot. In other respects he seems inclined to be impartial, recording several good and generous acts of Richard.

But there is one circumstance, which, besides the weakness and credulity of the man, renders his testimony exceedingly suspicious. After having said, that, *if he may speak truth in* Richard's *favour*,[56] he must own that, though small in stature and strength, Richard was a noble knight, and defended himself to the last breath with eminent valour, the monk suddenly turns, and apostrophizes Henry the Seventh, to whom he had dedicated his work, and whom he flatters to the best of his poor abilities; but, above all things, for having bestowed the name of Arthur on his eldest son, who, this injudicious and over-hasty prophet foresees, will restore the glory of his great ancestor of the same name. Had Henry christened his second son Merlin, I do not doubt but poor Rous would have had still more divine visions about Henry the Eighth, though born to shake half the pillars of credulity.

In short, no reliance can be had on an author of such a frame of mind, so removed from the scene of action, and so devoted to the Welsh intruder on the throne. Super-added to this incapacity and defects, he had prejudices or attachments of a private nature: he had singular affection for the Beauchamps, earls of Warwick,

56.   Attamen si ad ejus honorem veritatem dicam, p. 218.

104

zealous Lancastrians, and had written their lives. One capital crime that he imputes to Richard is the imprisonment of his mother-in-law, Ann Beauchamp countess of Warwick, mother of his queen. It does seem that this great lady was very hardly treated; but I have shown from the Chronicle of Croyland, that it was Edward the Fourth, not Richard, that stripped her of her possessions. She was widow too of that turbulent Warwick, the king-maker; and Henry the Seventh bore witness that she was faithfully loyal to Henry the Sixth. Still it seems extraordinary that the queen did not or could not obtain the enlargement of her mother. When Henry the Seventh attained the crown, she recovered her liberty and vast estates: yet young as his majesty was both in years and avarice, for this munificence took place in his third year, still he gave evidence of the falshood and rapacity of his nature; for though by act of parliament he cancelled the former act that had deprived her, *as against all reason, conscience, and course of nature, and contrary to the laws of God and man*,[57] and restored her possessions to her, this was but a farce, and like his wonted hypocrisy; for the very same year he obliged her to convey the whole estate to him, leaving her nothing but the manor of Sutton for her maintenance. Richard had married her daughter; but what claim had Henry to her inheritance? This attachment of Rous to the house of Beauchamp, and the dedication of his work to Henry, would make his testimony most suspicious, even if he had guarded his work within the rules of

57.   Vide Dugdale's Warwickshire in Beauchamp.

probability, and not rendered it a contemptible legend.

Every part of Richard's story is involved in obscurity: we neither know what natural children he had, nor what became of them. Sandford says, he had a daughter called Katherine, whom William Herbert earl of Huntingdon covenanted to marry, and to make her a fair and sufficient estate of certain of his manors to the yearly value of 200l. over and above all charges. As this lord received a confirmation of his title from Henry the Seventh, no doubt the poor young lady would have been sacrificed to that interest. But Dugdale seems to think she died before the nuptials were consummated: "whether this marriage took effect or not I cannot say; for sure it is that she died in her tender years."[58] Drake[59] affirms, that Richard knighted at York a natural son called Richard of Gloucester, and supposes it to be the same person of whom Peck has preserved so extraordinary an account.[60]* But never was a supposition worse grounded. The relation given by the latter of himself, was, that he never saw the king till the night before the battle of Bosworth; and that the king had not then acknowledged, but intended to acknowledge him, if victorious. The deep privacy in which this person had lived, demonstrates how severely the persecution had raged against all that were connected with Richard, and how little truth was to be expected from the writers on the other side. Nor could Peck's Richard Plantagenet be

58. Baronage, p. 258.
59. In his History of York.
60. See his Desiderata Curiosa.

the same person with Richard of Gloucester, for the former was never known till he discovered himself to Sir Thomas Moyle; and Hall says that king Richard's natural son was in the hands of Henry the Seventh.* Buck says, that Richard made his son Richard of Gloucester, captain of Calais; but it appers from Rymer's Foedera, that Richard's natural son, who was captain of Calais, was called John. None of these accounts accord with Peck's; nor, for want of knowing his mother, can we guess why king Richard was more secret on the birth of this son (if Peck's Richard Plantagenet was truly so) than on those of his other natural children. Perhaps the truest remark that can be made on this whole story is, that the avidity with which our historians swallowed one gross ill-concocted legend, prevented them from desiring or daring to sift a single part of it. If crumbs of truth are mingled with it, at least they are now undistinguishable in such a mass of error and improbability.*

It is evident from the conduct of Shakespeare, that the house of Tudor retained all their Lancastrian prejudices, even in the reign of queen Elizabeth. In his play of Richard the Third, he seems to deduce the woes of the house of York from the curses which queen Margaret had vented against them; and he could not give that weight to her curses, without supposing a right in her to utter them. This indeed is the authority which I do not pretend to combat. Shakespeare's immortal scenes will exist, when such poor arguments as mine are forgotten. Richard at least will be tried and executed on the stage, when his defence remains on some obscure shelf of a library. But while these pages may excite the curiosity of a day, it may not be unentertaining to observe, that there is another of Shakespeare's plays, that may be ranked among the historic, though not one of his numerous critics and commentators have discovered the drift of it; I mean *The Winter Evening's Tale*, which was certainly intended (in compliment to queen Elizabeth) as an indirect apology for her mother Anne Boleyn.* The address of the poet appears no where to more advantage. The subject was too delicate to be exhibited on the stage without a veil; and it was too recent, and touched the queen too nearly, for the bard to have ventured so home an allusion on any other ground than compliment. The unreasonable jealousy of Leontes, and his violent conduct in consequence, form a true portrait of Henry the Eighth, who generally made the law the engine of his boisterous passions. Not only the general plan of the story is most applicable, but several passages are so marked, that they touch the real history nearer than the fable. Hermione on her trial says,

——for honour,
'Tis a derivative from me to mine,
And only that I stand for.

This seems to be taken from the very letter of Anne Boleyn to the king before her execution, where she pleads for the infant princess his daughter. Mamillius, the young prince, an unnecessary character, dies in his infancy; but it confirms the allusion, as queen Anne, before Elizabeth, bore a still-born son. But the most striking passage, and which had nothing to do in the tragedy, but as it pictured Elizabeth, is, where Paulina, describing the new-born princess, and her likeness to her father, says, *she has the very trick of his frown*. There is one sentence indeed so applicable, both to Elizabeth and her father, that I should suspect the poet inserted it after her death. Paulina, speaking of the child, tells the king,

───'Tis yours;
And might we lay the old proverb to your charge,
So like you, 'tis the worse—

The Winter Evening's Tale was therefore in reality a second part of Henry the Eighth.*

With regard to Jane Shore, I have already shown that it was her connection with the marquis Dorset, not with lord Hastings, which drew on her the resentment of Richard. When an event is thus wrested to serve the purpose of a party, we ought to be very cautious how we trust an historian, who is capable of employing truth only as cement in a fabric of fiction. Sir Thomas More tells us, that Richard pretended Jane "was of councell with the lord Hastings to destroy him; and in conclusion, when no colour could fasten upon these matters, then he layd seriously to her charge what she could not deny," namely her adultery; "and for this cause, as a godly continent prince, cleane and faultlesse of himself, sent out of heaven into this vicious world for the amendment of mens manners, he caused the bishop of London to put her to open penance."

This sarcasm on Richard's morals would have had more weight, if the author had before confined himself to deliver nothing but the precise truth. He does not seem to be more exact in what relates to the penance itself. Richard, by his proclamation, taxed mistress Shore with plotting treason in confederacy with the marquis Dorset. Consequently, it was not from defect of proof of her being accomplice with lord Hastings that she was put to open penance. If Richard had any hand in that sentence, it was, because he *had* proof of her plotting with the marquis. But I doubt, and with some reason, whether her penance was inflicted by Richard. We have seen that he acknowledged at least two natural children; and Sir Thomas More hints that Richard was far from being remarkable for his chastity. Is it therefore probable, that he acted so silly a farce as to make his brother's mistress do penance? Most of the charges on Richard are so idle, that instead of being an able and artful usurper, as his antagonists allow, he must have been a weaker hypocrite than ever attempted to wrest a sceptre out of the hands of a legal possessor.

It is more likely that the churchmen were the authors of Jane's penance; and that Richard, interested to manage that body, and provoked by her connection with so capital an enemy as Dorset, might give her up, and permit the clergy (who probably had burned incense to her in her prosperity) to revenge his quarrel. My reason for this opinion is grounded on a letter of Richard extant in the Museum, by which it appears that the fair, unfortunate, and amiable Jane (for her virtues far outweighed her frailty) being a prisoner, by Richard's order, in Ludgate, had captivated the king's sollicitor, who contracted to marry her. Here follows the letter:

By the KING

"Right reverend fadre in God. &c. Signifying unto you, that it is shewed unto us, that our servaunt and solicitor, Thomas Lynom, merveillously blinded and abused with the late (wife) of Willm Shore, now being in Ludgate by oure commandment, hath made contract of matrymony with hir (as it is said) and entendith, to our full grete merveile, to procede to th'effect of the same. We for many causes wold be sory that hee soo shuide be disposed. Pray you therefore to send for him, and in that ye goodly may, exhorte and sture hym to the contrarye. And if ye finde him utterly set for to marye hur, and noen otherwise will be advertised, then (if it may stand with the lawe of the churche) We be content (the tyme of mariage deferred to our comyng next to London) that upon sufficient suertie founde of hure good abering, ye doo send for hure keeper, and discharge him of our said commandment by warrant of these, committing hur to the rule and guiding of hure fadre, or any othre by your discretion in the mene season.
                    Yeven, &c.
"To the right reverend fadre in God, &c. the bishop of Lincoln, our chauncellour."

It appears from this letter, that Richard thought it indecent for his solicitor to marry a woman who had suffered public punishment for adultery, and who was confined by his command – but where is the tyrant to be found in this paper? Or, what prince ever spoke of such a scandal, and what is stronger, of such contempt of his authority, with so much lenity and temper? He enjoins his chancellor to dissuade the sollicitor from the match — but should he persist — a tyrant would have ordered the sollicitor to prison too — but Richard — Richard, if his servant will not be dissuaded, allows the match; and in the mean time commits Jane — to whose custody? — Her own father's. I cannot help thinking that some holy person had been her persecutor, and not so patient and gentle a king. And I believe so, because of the salvo for the church: "Let them be married," says Richard, "if it may stand with the lawe of the churche."

From the proposed marriage, one should at first conclude that Shore, the former husband of Jane, was dead; but by the king's query, whether the marriage would be lawful? and by her being called in the letter *the late wife of William Shore*, not *of the late William Shore*, I should suppose that her husband was living, and that the penance itself was the consequence of a suit preferred by him to the ecclesiastic court for divorce.* If the injured husband ventured, on the death of Edward the Fourth, to petition to be separated from his wife, it was natural enough for the church to proceed farther, and enjoin her to perform penance, especially when they fell in with the king's resentment to her. Richard's proclamation and the letter above-recited seem to point out this account of Jane's misfortunes; the letter implying, that Richard doubted whether her divorce was so complete as to leave her at liberty to take another husband. As we hear no more of the marriage, and as Jane to her death retained the name of Shore, my solution is corroborated; the

112

chancellor-bishop, no doubt, going more roundly to work than the king had done. Nor, however Sir Thomas More reviles Richard for his cruel usage of mistress Shore, did either of the succeeding kings redress her wrongs, though she lived to the eighteenth year of Henry the Eighth. She had sown her good deeds, her good offices, her alms, her charities, in a court. Not one took root; nor did the ungrateful soil repay her a grain of relief in her penury and comfortless old age.

I have thus gone through the several accusations against Richard; and have shown that they rest on the slightest and most suspicious ground, if they rest on any at all. I have proved that they ought to be reduced to the sole authorities of Sir Thomas More and Henry the Seventh; the latter interested to blacken and misrepresent every action of Richard; and perhaps driven to father on him even his own crimes. I have proved that More's account cannot be true. I have shown that the writers, contemporary with Richard, either do not accuse him, or give their accusations as mere vague and uncertain reports: and what is as strong, the writers next in date, and who wrote the earliest after the events are said to have happened, assert little or nothing from their own information, but adopt the very words of Sir Thomas More, who was absolutely mistaken or misinformed.

For the sake of those who have a mind to canvass this subject, I will recapitulate the most material arguments that tend to disprove what has been asserted; but as I attempt not to affirm what *did* happen in a period that will still remain very obscure, I flatter myself that I shall not be thought either fantastic or paradoxical, for not blindly adopting an improbable tale, which our historians have never given themselves the trouble to examine.

What mistakes I may have made myself, I shall be willing to acknowledge; what weak reasoning, to give up: but I shall not think that a long chain of arguments, of proofs and probabilities, is confuted at once, because some single fact may be found erroneous. Much less shall I be disposed to take notice of detached or trifling cavils. The work itself is but an inquiry into a short portion of our annals. I shall be content, if I have informed or amused my readers, or thrown any light on so clouded a scene; but I cannot be of opinion that a period thus distant deserves to take up more time than I have already bestowed upon it.

It seems then to me to appear,

That Fabian and the authors of the Chronicle of Croyland, who were contemporaries with Richard, charge him directly with none of the crimes, since imputed to him, and disculpate him of others.

That John Rous, the third contemporary, could know the facts he alledges but by hearsay, confounds the dates of them, dedicated his work to Henry the Seventh, and is an author to whom no credit is due, from the lies and fables with which his work is stuffed.

That we have no authors, who lived near the time, but Lancastrian authors, who wrote to flatter Henry the Seventh, or who spread the tales which he invented.

114

That the murder of prince Edward, son of Henry the Sixth, was committed by king Edward's servants, and is imputed to Richard by no contemporary.

That Henry the Sixth was found dead in the Tower; that it was not known how he came by his death; and that it was against Richard's interest to murder him.

That the duke of Clarence was defended by Richard; that the parliament petitioned for his execution; that no author of the time is so absurd as to charge Richard with being the executioner; and that king Edward took the deed wholly on himself.

That Richard's stay at York on his brother's death had no appearance of a design to make himself king.

That the ambition of the queen, who attempted to usurp the government, contrary to the then established custom of the realm, gave the first provocation to Richard and the princes of the blood to assert their rights; and that Richard was sollicited by the duke of Buckingham to vindicate those rights.

That the preparation of an armed force under earl Rivers, the seizure of the Tower and treasure, and the equipment of a fleet, by the marquis Dorset, gave occasion to the princes to imprison the relations of the queen; and that, though they were put to death without trial (the only cruelty which is *proved* on Richard) it was consonant to the manners of that barbarous and turbulent age, and not till after the queen's party had taken up arms.

That the execution of lord Hastings, who had first engaged with Richard against the queen, and whom Sir Thomas More confesses Richard was *lothe to lose*, can be accounted for by nothing but absolute necessity, and the law of self-defence.

That Richard's assumption of the protectorate was in every respect agreable to the laws and usage; was probably bestowed on him by the universal consent of the council and peers, and was a strong indication that he had then no thought of questioning the right of his nephew.

That the tale of Richard aspersing the chastity of his own mother is incredible; it appearing that he lived with her in perfect harmony, and lodged with her in her palace at that very time.

That it is as little credible that Richard gained the crown by a sermon of Dr. Shaw, and a speech of the duke of Buckingham, if the people only laughed at those orators.

That there had been a precontract or marriage between Edward the Fourth and lady Eleanor Talbot; and that Richrd's claim to the crown was founded on the illegitimacy of Edward's children.

That a convention of the nobility, clergy, and people invited him to accept the crown on that title.

That the ensuing parliament ratified the act of the convention, and confirmed the bastardy of Edward's children.

That nothing can be more improbable than Richard's having taken no measures before he left London, to have his nephews murdered, if he had had any such intention.

That the story of Sir James Tirrel, as related by Sir Thomas More, is a notorious falshood; Sir James Tirrel being at that time master of the horse, in which capacity he had walked at Richard's coronation.

That Tirrel's jealousy of Sir Richard Ratcliffe is another palpable falshood; Tirrel being already preferred, and Ratcliffe absent.

That all that relates to Sir Robert Brakenbury is no less false: Brakenbury either being too good a man to die for a tyrant or murderer, or too bad a man to have refused being his accomplice.

That Sir Thomas More and lord Bacon both confess that many doubted, whether the two princes were murdered in Richard's days or not; and it certainly never was proved that they were murdered by Richard's order.

That Sir Thomas More relied on nameless and uncertain authority; that it appears by dates and facts that his authorities were bad and false; that if Sir James Tirrel and Dighton had really committed the murder and confessed it, and if Perkin Warbeck had made a voluntary, clear, and probable confession of his imposture, there could have remained no doubt of the murder.

That Green, the nameless page, and Will Slaughter, having never been questioned about the murder, there is no reason to believe what is related of them in the supposed tragedy.

That Sir James Tirrel not being attainted on

the death of Richard, but having, on the contrary, been employed in great services by Henry the Seventh, it is not probable that he was one of the murderers. That lord Bacon owning that Tirrel's confession did not please the king so well as Dighton's; that Tirrel's imprisonment and execution some years afterwards for a new treason, of which we have no evidence, and which appears to have been mere suspicion, destroy all probability of his guilt in the supposed murder of the children.

That the impunity of Dighton, if really guilty, was scandalous; and can only be accounted for on the supposition of his being a false witness to serve Henry's cause against Perkin Warbeck.

That the silence of the two archbishops, and Henry's not daring to specify the murder of the princes in the act of attainder against Richard, wears all the appearance of their not having been murdered.

That Richard's tenderness and kindness to the earl of Warwick, proceeding so far as to proclaim him his successor, betrays no symptom of that cruel nature, which would not stick at assassinating any competitor.

That it is indubitable that Richard's first idea was to keep the crown but till Edward the Fifth should attain the age of twenty-four.

That with this view he did *not* create his own son prince of Wales till after he had proved the bastardy of his brother's children.

That there is no proof that those children were murdered.

That Richard made, or intended to make, his nephew Edward the Fifth walk at his coronation.

That there is strong presumption from the parliament-roll and from the Chronicle of Croyland, that both princes were living some time after Sir Thomas More fixes the date of their deaths.

That when his own son was dead, Richard was so far from intending to get rid of his wife, that he proclaimed his nephews, first the earl of Warwick, and then the earl of Lincoln, his heirs apparent.

That there is not the least probability of his having poisoned his wife, who died of a languishing distemper: that no proof was ever pretended to be given of it; that a bare supposition of such a crime, without proofs or very strong presumptions, is scarce ever to be credited.

That he seems to have had no intention of marrying his niece, but to have amused her with the hopes of that match, to prevent her marrying Richmond.

That Buck would not have dared to quote her letter as extant in the earl of Arundel's library, if it had not been there: that others of Buck's assertions having been corroborated by subsequent discoveries, leave no doubt of his veracity on this; and that that letter disculpates Richard from poisoning his wife; and only shews the impatience of his niece to be queen.

That it is probable the queen-dowager knew her second son was living, and connived at the appearance of Lambert Simnel, to feel the temper of the nation.

That Henry the Seventh certainly thought that she and the earl of Lincoln were privy to the existence of Richard duke of York, and that Henry lived in terror of his appearance.

That the different conduct of Henry with regard to Lambert Simnel and Perkin Warbeck, implies how different an opinion he had of them; that, in the first case, he used the most natural and most rational methods to prove him an impostor; whereas his whole behaviour in Perkin's case was mysterious, and betrayed his belief or doubt that Warbeck was the true duke of York.

That it was morally impossible for the duchess of Burgundy at the distance of twenty-seven years to instruct a Flemish lad so perfectly in all that had passed in the court of England, that he would not have been detected in few hours.

That she could not inform him, nor could he know, what had passed in the Tower, unless he was the true duke of York.

That if he was not the true duke of York, Henry had nothing to do but to confront him with Tirrel and Dighton, and the imposture must have been discovered.

That Perkin, never being confronted with the queen-dowager, and the princesses her daughters, proved that Henry did not dare to trust to their acknowledging him.

That if he was not the true duke of York, he might have been detected by not knowing the queens and princesses, if shown to him without his being told who they were.

That it is not pretended that Perkin ever failed in language, accent, or circumstances; and that his likeness to Edward the Fourth is allowed.

That there are gross and manifest blunders in his pretended confession.

That Henry was so afraid of not ascertaining a good account of the purity of his English accent, that he makes him learn English twice over.

That lord Bacon did not dare to adhere to this ridiculous account; but forges another, though in reality, not much more credible.

That a number of Henry's best friends, as the lord chamberlain, who placed the crown on his head, knights of the garter, and men of the fairest characters, being persuaded that Perkin was the true duke of York, and dying for that belief, without recanting, makes it very rash to deny that he was so.

That the proclamation in Rymer's Foedera against Jane Shore, for plotting with the marquis Dorset, not with lord Hastings, destroys all the credit of Sir Thomas More, as to what relates to the latter peer.

In short, that Henry's character, as we have received it from his own apologists, is so much worse and more hateful than Richard's, that we may well believe Henry invented and propagated by far the greater part of the slanders against Richard: that Henry, not Richard, probably put to death the true duke of York, as he did the earl of Warwick: and that we are not certain whether Edward the Fifth was murdered; nor, if he was, by whose order he was murdered.

After all that has been said, it is scarce necessary to add a word on the supposed discovery that was made of the skeletons of the two young princes, in the reign of Charles the Second. Two skeletons found in that dark abyss of so many secret transactions, with no marks to ascertain the time, the age of their interment, can certainly verify nothing. We must believe both princes died there, before we can believe that their bones were found there: and upon what that belief can be founded, or how we shall cease to doubt whether Perkin Warbeck was not one of those children, I am at a loss to guess.

As little is it requisite to argue on the grants made by Richard the Third to his supposed accomplices in that murder, because the argument will serve either way. It was very natural that they, who had tasted most of Richard's bounty, should be suspected as the instruments of his crimes. But till it can be proved that those crimes were committed, it is in vain to bring evidence to show who assisted him in perpetrating them. For my own part, I know not what to think of the death of Edward the Fifth: I can neither entirely acquit Richard of it, nor condemn him; because there are no proofs on either side; and though a court of justice would, from that defect of evidence, absolve him; opinion may fluctuate backwards and forwards, and at last remain in suspense.

For the younger brother, the balance seems to incline greatly on the side of Perkin Warbeck, as the true duke of York; and if one was saved, one knows not how or why to believe that Richard destroyed only the elder.

We must leave this whole story dark, though not near so dark as we found it: and it is perhaps as wise to be uncertain on one portion of our history, as to believe so much as is believed in all histories, though very probably as falsely delivered to us, as the period which we have here been examining.

FINIS

ADDITION

The following notice, obligingly communicated to me by Mr. Stanley, came too late to be inserted in the body of the work, and yet ought not to be omitted.

After the death of Perkin Warbeck, his widow, the lady Catherine Gordon, daughter of the earl of Huntley, from her exquisite beauty, and upon account of her husband called *The white rose of Scotland*, was married to Sir Matthew Cradock, and is buried with him in Herbert's isle in Swansea church in Wales, where their tomb is still to be seen, with this inscription in ancient characters:

"Here lies Sr Mathie Cradok knight, sume time deputie unto the right honorable Charles Erle of Worcets in the countie of Glamorgan, R. Attor. G. R. Chauncelor of the same, steward of Gower and Hilvei, and mi ladie Katerin his wife."

They had a daughter Mary, who was married to Sir Edward Herbert, son of the first earl of Pembroke; and from that match are descended the earls of Pembroke and countess of Powis, Hans Stanley, Esq; George Rice, Esq; &c.

SUPPLEMENT
TO THE HISTORIC DOUBTS
ON THE LIFE AND REIGN OF
KING RICHARD THE THIRD

With Remarks on some Answers that have
been made to that Work

> Quoth Hudibras, I now perceive
> You are no conjurer, by your leave.
> That paltry story is untrue,
> And forg'd to cheat such gulls as you.
> *Hud. part II, cant. 3.*

SUPPLEMENT TO THE
HISTORIC DOUBTS

When I published my doubts on the reign of king Richard the third, I concluded, from the obscurity of the subject, and from my own want of abilities, and superficial knowledge of our story, that men of deeper reading and masters of sounder reasoning would easily overthrow my arguments [though offered but as doubts], and would destroy what foundations I had pretended to lay, though corroborated by some facts, and established on some new and not totally despicable materials. To this humiliation, for the sake of truth, and of clearing up a very dark and intricate period, I was ready to submit, I wished to see a foolish and absurd tale removed from the pages of our gravest historians; and flattered myself, that not only the ridiculous and incoherent parts of the legend would be given up by men of sense, but that some able writer would deign to state the whole matter in so clear and consistent a manner, that not only my doubts [which indeed are of little importance to any body] would be removed, but that the history of that period would receive such satisfactory, at least probable lights, as would prevent the reign of Richard from disgracing our annals by an intrusion of mob-stories and childish improbabilities, which at present in our best historians place that reign on a level with the story of Jack the giant-killer.

The remoteness of the time in question gave me those hopes. I should not indeed have been so weak as to flatter myself, while the spirit of party is in full vigour, that any concessions on later reigns would be made to a candid enquirer after truth. That perverse spirit, wilfully blind, adheres obstinately to the sacred disputes of our ancestors, and renders our history but a more bulky compilation of controversial pamphlets. To this hour the reigns of the Stuarts, the most ignominious period of our annals, are defended, justified, varnished, nay panegyricized, by able writers as well as by the most contemptible; as if that disgraceful succession was the favourite portion of our history with our favourite historians. Elizabeth and Cromwell, who, with all their faults, raised the dignity and honour of our country, and made it the terror of foreign nations, consoling us at least by national glory for national servitude, are depressed and vilified, in compliment to a despicable race, who with equal ambition were destitute of every talent to support it, and who naturally sunk in the esteem of Europe, as fast as they lost the hearts and respect of their own subjects.

The satisfaction I expected, nobody has deigned to give me; and were I so idly vain as to conclude, because my arguments have *not* been answered, that therefore they are unanswerable, I might indulge myself in the delusion of thinking that I have done some service to our history in clearing away a load of rubbish, that had obtained a prescriptive right of lying in the way of our historians, merely because it had been carelessly thrown there by writers, whose very dirt and mortar passed for buildings. Far from such presumption, I am persuaded that my

128

doubts have not seemed to deserve an answer from those who are capable of giving one. To such men I must have appeared a paradoxical writer; and the story of Richard the third with all its absurdities is still deemed authentic, *because* Sir Thomas More, who wrote it in his youth, proved afterwards a very great man; and *because* lord Bacon, who copied it afterwards into a fulsome panegyric, and who however corrected the original silly account without making it consistent, was the founder of modern philosophy, and as bright a genius as ever shone in the orb of literature. Nobody respects such great names more than I do. Yet, if whatever fell from the pen of More be holy writ, why should we not embrace his religion as well as his history? In his graver years he fell into all the follies of enthusiasm and bigotry, which he had ridiculed in his youth. I have shown many palpable falsities in his history. It is a poor refuge to set up his name against his mistakes: and methinks of all men living a sceptic philosopher is the last one should expect to find pinning his faith on the sleeve of reverend authority. Lord Bacon is still less entitled to our implicit assent. To say nothing of his slavish flattery to his living masters, can that man be received as an historian of unquestionable veracity, who has laboured to consecrate the crimes of Henry the seventh, and held forth the meanest tyrant as the model of political wisdom? Such historians stain the records of truth, and no talents can rescue their characters from contempt. To enshrine guilt, is sinning against virtue and wounding posterity. Tyrants are lulled with the hope of finding similar panegyrists: and history is the tribunal at which all princes must

129

appear, shall the bad dare to hope for advocates at that bar? Shall Henry the seventh of England and Henry the fourth of France receive the same palm from the same judicatory?

I am sorry to be forced to repeat these arguments, having mentioned them before; but such magic is there in great names, and it is so commode to use them instead of reasons, that one is obliged to expose the futility of such authorities when they are made the standard of truth against truth itself.

When I said that my arguments had not received an answer, I did not mean that my book had not been answered. It has been treated like the works of much better authors, and been attended both with that abuse and compliment that are essentially necessary to flatter a writer with the hopes of not being forgotten. I am very grateful for both; and equally satisfied with having offended some, and pleased others of my readers.

The first marks of disapprobation were conveyed in the Critical Review. I was severely reproved by that monthly court for not having taken due notice of Mr. Guthrie's History of England.* The charge I acknowledge was just. When I examined the story of Richard the third, it is true that I consulted the living works of dead authors, not the dead works of living authors. And it ought to be some palliation of my offence, that I not only had never seen Mr. Guthrie's History of England, but had never met with a single person that had read it. It had remained a profound secret to mortal eyes; or was consumed by those all-devouring enemies of the ingenious, time and the oven. However, I am sincerely sorry for my neglect; and the more so, as I find by the review, that my misfortune did not consist in differing with Mr. Guthrie, but in happening to be of the same opinion. It seems, Mr. Guthrie, long before the appearance of my Doubts, had condemned great part of the traditional history of Richard as a fable. It was therefore presumptuous in me to be as sagacious as so inimitable a writer; or a grievous affront not to acknowledge that he had previously started the same opinion. Why he should be amibitious of singularity I do not know. The more persons see through an absurdity, the more probable it is that the absurdity exists. Indeed, when an author has compiled our annals, I find he looks on the whole history of England as his property. It is an invasion of his freehold to contest a single fact that he has occupied. Mr. Guthrie and Mr. Hume assert their right to the whole manour. Mr. Guthrie will not suffer me to agree with him, nor Mr. Hume to disagree with him. When they have adjusted their title between themselves, I will swear to the lawful monarch – in the mean time I hope I may be allowed to treat one of them at least as a pretender.

To the abuse with which those literary in-quisitors the reviewers have honoured me, I acquiesce with gratitude. Not only in the case in question, but on other occasions, they have obliged me with that censure which bad au-thors, turned to critics, are so apt to pass on better writers than themselves. I have had the satisfaction of seeing my trifling writings rise in the favour of the public, in proportion as they have been condemned by the judicious gentle-men who are so laborious and kind as for a shilling a month to inform their humble auditors what they should think of every book, which the latter never read. May it ever be my fate [should I again attempt to amuse the public] to pass through the innoxious flames of such criticism; secure of losing no particle of my little merit by being grinned and mouthed at by as grotesque imps, as those that pipe and drum in the pictures of Teniers, to divert, one should think, rather than terrify saint Antony!

As I look on abuse as a flattering tribute paid by wounded or impotent enemeies, so I am apt to suspect that when an author is profuse of compliments to his adversary, he really but laughs in secret at his opponent's abilities, and exalts them officiously, in order to render his own triumph more conspicuous.

Next to the capital offence of not having consulted Mr. Guthrie's departed history, I seem to have disgusted him or his champions by having treated disrespectfully some ancient chroniclers, particularly

"Those classics of an age that knew of none,"

Ingulphus, Matthew Paris, William of Malmesbury, Henry of Huntingdon, and Hoveden; though by the way I have never mentioned them. It would puzzle me, I am told, to produce a Latin historian *now alive*, superior to William of Malmesbury, with regard to spirit, sentiment, and authenticity, nay, in the beauty of composition and elegance of diction. It would puzzle me indeed; as, except Buonamici's, I did not know that our modern histories were written in Latin. If they are, I offer them as an oblation one and all to the shades of the elegant Ingulphus, and as elegant Mr. Guthrie, the latter of whom for aught I know may have written his history in Latin too. Nay, from one passage, I have some suspicion that he may have written it in Greek, the thought being truly Anacreontic. He suspects that the duke of Clarence was not drowned in a butt of malmsey, but died of drinking that wine. The figure is a little bold, and above the common pitch of an antiquary: but poets and antiquaries are equally adventurous in their conjectures; and as the criticism is excellent, no doubt it will meet with proper respect from all those learned persons who shall re-write our history.

If it would not be trifling with my readers, I would mention another passage containing a thought not less new. The critic says, that sir Thomas More never did deserve *but in death* the name he has obtained for sincerity and honesty. How a man can deserve the character of honesty in death, who never deserved it in his life, is totally past my comprehension.

Having for some pages resented my agreement with him, Mr. Guthrie takes a short turn, and undertakes the condemnation of Richard against me, for fear I should not be in the wrong both ways. His chief argument against himself and me, *that Tirrel certainly murdered the two princes*, is drawn from the propriety of his being a person fit for the office. How is this made out? I had shown, that, instead of being the low tool described by sir Thomas More, Tirrel was a man of great note, and in high employment. How does Mr. Guthrie destroy this argument? By producing a commission to prove that Tirrel was a much greater man than I had represented him, having even in king Edward's time been appointed one of the commissioners for exercising the office of high constable of England. I thankfully accept this evidence against sir Thomas More: it certainly does demonstrate that Tirrel was not a mean fellow, a comrade of the page, who sir Thomas says recommended him as a fit instrument for a secret assassination. – Now let us see how I can defend Mr. Guthrie and myself against Mr. Guthrie.

A clause, says Mr. Guthrie, was omitted in the renewal of the patent which allowed to the commissioners clerks to take down the minutes of the proceedings, &c. *Had not Tirrel*, continues he, *with such a commission, some reason to think he was safe against all legal impeachments even in the following reign?* As all Richard's acts were in the following reign deemed the acts of an usurper, and consequently cancelled in effect, I should think not. But I cannot from what Tirrel might think deduce any manner of argument for showing that he was the murderer! But, says Mr. Guthrie, by the omission of clerks, Tirrel, or whoever the murderer was, had no occasion to call in any assistance or clerks. As I am defending Mr. Guthrie as well as myself, he will allow us to say, that instead of argument, this is downright nonsense. Does the command over assistants aid or defeat murder? Or, because a commissioner has clerks, is he obliged by law to enjoin them co-operation in murder? *By having no clerks,* says he, *he had no occasion to call in any assistance.* Suppose my lord commissioner Tirrel had had clerks, does Mr. Guthrie think they would have sued him for not employing them in assassination? But here are words more strange; *Tirrel, or whoever the murderer was.* Mr. Guthrie, then, it seems, doubts after all whether Tirrel was the real criminal or not. Observe how that very doubt makes him flounder out of one absurdity into another. By Tirrel's having no clerks, the murderer, *whoever he was*, had no occasion to call in any assistance: ergo, if Tirrel was *not* the murderer, whoever was had no occasion to call in any assistance, because the lord high constable pro tempore happened to have no clerks. Thus do materials but serve to overset a head that knows not how to digest them! And this is the historian that I am censured for not having consulted!

Mr. Guthrie is much happier in the application of materials that he has *not* met with. *The lady Eleanor Butler*, says he, *acquitted the king of any promise in open court*. This is a bold assertion. I would ask with submission, in what court that cause was tried, and where the records exists?* So indefatigable a hunter after ancient game, no doubt can inform us where he discovered the minutes of the trial. Sure he did not adopt this random information from the authors he condemns, and who, he says,[1] *wrote under the influence of the house of Lancaster. Nothing then was thought too mean, however false it might be, for flattering the reigning powers*. If Mr. Guthrie is master of more authentic intelligence on this article, he will no doubt produce it.

In one point I acknowledge he has corrected me justly. I mentioned the duke of Albany being with Richard at York, as a presumption that Richard was on good terms with the court of Scotland; whereas, says Mr. Guthrie, and he is in the right, the duke of Albany lived then in exile, being on bad terms with his brother

1.   Vide Critical Review, No. 145, p. 121, in the note from Guthrie.

135

James the third.* I beg the reader to substract as much weight from the chain of my argument, as this mistake had made on his mind. Let this recantation evince that I am neither obstinate nor incorrigible. Had I met with either one fact or argument more in the writings of my opponents of equal weight, I should have yielded with the same facility. To adhere to what one cannot maintain, especially on so unimportant a subject as the history of Richard, would betray a vanity that expects the world should acquiesce in our weaknesses or prejudices, and a mind too disingenuous to acknowledge itself capable of mistakes.

My next adversary was a very civil gentleman, who did me the honour of answering my doubts in a volume as large as my own. He paid me so many compliments, that I beg he will draw upon me for the full debt, whenever he has occasion for the like number.*

Not so the third. Determined on the ruin of my work, and at the same time descreetly allowing sufficient intervals to his readers to digest his censures, he retailed them in that vehicle of universal and distributive justice, the *London Chronicle*.* His friends, he said, had indeed persuaded him to collect the scattered leaves into a just volume – and he flattered the world with some hopes of his compliance. Might I presume to subscribe their petition, I would entreat him to indulge their wishes; especially as he broke off exactly at that part of my work, in which I had placed the strength of my argument. Content however with the sample he had given of his abilities, he concluded the world would give him credit from what he had done, for what he was able to do. As a specimen of those abilities, I shall from many of equally cogent logic select one instance. It will suffice to show why I am unwilling to encounter so tremendous a foe; at the same time that I do not feel myself sufficiently warmed by his passionate expressions to answer them with equal fury. Perhaps this author too may have written his history of England, and cannot forgive my not having quoted it. From the pains-taking compiler, who is twenty-five years in composing half a reign, to the garreteer, who transfuses old historians into weekly numbers as fast as his printer can dispatch them, the cohort of English historians is become so extensive a fraternity, that life is not long enough, though we should do nothing but read our own story in their various modifications of it. The passage I hinted at is in the Chronicle of March 12, 1768. The critic has discovered there that when the historian says prince Edward [son of Henry 6th] was murdered by the *servants* of Edward the fourth, we may easily suppose he meant the king's *brothers*; for, says he, *judiciously*, are not the *king's brothers* the king's servants? Let me ask this angry and shrewd person, whether, if he was to read in the Daily Advertiser that his majesty went to the opera attended by his *servants*, he should understand that his majesty's royal *brothers* walked before his chair? I have heard that omne majus continet in se minus; but this is the first time I have seen that proposition inverted. – It was a cruel friend that advised this author to reprint such lucubrations!

Having dispatched these skirmishers with perhaps more notice than they deserved, I must now turn to another kind of adversary, to one from whom I differ with regret, and whose

137

talents I cannot encounter without fear: one
whose knowledge is only excelled by his power
of employing it: whose sagacity may nod,
though it cannot be imposed upon; and who is
more able to defend a bad cause, than I am to do
justice to a good one: one who could sip the
muddy streams of Ingulphus and Hoveden,
without being intoxicated by them; and who, if
it would have served any political purpose,
could have cast such a plausible veil over the
deformities of Richard, that my attempt to
rescue his character from obloquy had been
needless and impotent, when compared with
what his masterly hand would have performed.
Grieved I am therefore to think that what his
haste made him neglect, he should not suffer to
be executed in however inferior a manner by
me. Yet what makes *him* averse from seeing *any*
king whitewashed? Have I violated the ashes of
his favourite martyr, I mean as they are enshrined in his volumes? The profane Mrs.
Macaulay has proved the gross insincerity of
that monarch. She has detected our author's
beloved Clarendon in numberless wilful falsehoods, – nay, she has not treated our author
himself with much ceremony. Yet she remains
unanswered; and her arguments, built on records and incontestable authorities, seem like a
rock to defy his assaults. My poor tribute to
royalty is the only mite that is rejected. A notice
however I cannot but esteem a singular honour,
as, amidst a host of adversaries of various sorts,
I am the only one to whom I think our author has
ever deigned to make a reply. In truth, if the
passages I am going to examine are to be
regarded as a specimen of his polemic talents, he
will forgive me I hope for saying, that he was

not only in the right to select the weakest of his adversaries, but prudent in abstaining from a warfare in which his greatest force does not seem to lie.

After the first gush of opponents whom I have mentioned, my Doubts seemed to have nothing farther to fear but oblivion. I thought my work as much forgotten, as I had forgot my adversaries, I neither cared about them nor king Richard. How was I surprised the other day on receiving a present of a French Swiss journal from the learned[2] author himself, in which the first thing in the book was a criticism on my Doubts.* – I call it criticism in deference to the author, though the whole, like other reviews, is chiefly composed of extracts from my work; and, unlike other reviews, of such a torrent of encomiums on myself, as made me blush for the mistaken good-nature of the author, and for my own demerit, which is ill entitled to such incense. Indeed, any vanity I might have conceived from this panegyric was greatly lowered by a passage at the end of the book, in which the author modestly owns that he does not much admire the works of doctor Swift. Could I be greatly flattered with the approbation of a gentleman who has so little taste as to dislike doctor Swift and to admire me? How qualified is this kind person to fit in judgment on books, who gives such a criterion of his distinguishing faculties!

If I found myself overwhelmed with praise, I was not less astonished to find at the end of his criticism two or three pages drawn up by Mr.

2. Monf. Diverdun, author of Mémoires litteraires de la Grande Bretagne pour les années 1767, 1768.

Hume in answer to my Doubts, and bestowed on the journalist to help him in pronouncing sentence. He pronounces it accordingly, and declares me guilty of specious but false reasoning, and decides the victory in favour of Mr. Hume on the evidence collected from the latter's own notes.

The notes thus crept into the world are in French. Many months ago Mr. Hume gave me a sight of them in English, and I then told him what I must repeat now, that I thought I never saw more unsubstantial arguments. As he is of a different opinion, and as I am now at liberty to take them to pieces, I shall make bold to show, that they are not only no answer to my reasonings, which remain in full force, but that, if they are the best confutation Mr. Hume can make of my book, it had been wiser to let it sink or swim as it could, instead of heaping conjectures on improbabilities, and thereby leading our readers to see, that he not only avoided giving answers to my strongest arguments, but had rashly taken up an idle story without examination, and now is at a loss how to defend it.*

Before I enter on the discussion of Mr. Hume's notes, I must make one or two short observations. Having remarked how shallow the authorities were on which the history of Richard is built, I thought myself warranted to call much of it in question. Buck, Carte, and it seems Mr. Guthrie, had preceded me in rejecting the received account. Some new lights had accidentally flowed in. Still I proposed my sentiments but as *doubts* – and yet have been told that I have not *proved* my hypothesis. If I had *proved* it, I should not have *doubted*. My adversaries on the other side seem to think that assertions and repetitions will serve for proofs, where facts and reasons are wanting. The best reasoner and greatest sceptic amongst them has for once listed under such mob-banners, and coolly retails the very same kind of logic against me, that has so often been wasted in vain against himself. I own there is much difference between us; our abilities are as unequal as our bodily prowess: a feather may fell me; he can resist a broad-sword.

My next observation is, that Mr. Hume rests the whole of his confutation on the single fact, the murder of the children. Whether he allows that I have cleared Richard's character from the other murders, he leaves me uncertain. What does this silence imply? Am I to infer from it that he gives up all the rest, though he had adopted into his history many of those idle tales? Or am I to conclude that he despises my arguments? But so he does with regard to Perkin Warbeck. He endeavours to establish that imposture, but does not attempt to refute the reasons I have brought to support Perkin's being the true duke of York. I challenged him to reconcile the contradictions in the story: he reverts to great names, as if names were arguments. Are all the murders charged on Richard supported by one and the same authority? Does Mr. Hume think that, if he proves one, all the rest follow of course? Or does he hope to rehabilitate the credit of his history, by attempting to show that in one point he has not been mistaken or lightly credulous? I must leave it to his own candour to answer these questions – and shall now show, that if he has no better arguments in store than what he has bounteously bestowed on his friend the journalist, or thought good enough for both him and me, the assumption of Perkin Warbeck being the true son of Edward the fourth, will gain new strength by the trifling arguments so great a man as Mr. Hume has been reduced to bring on the contrary side of the question.

The first note says that, *in general there reigns a great obscurity in the circumstances of the wars between the two roses.* * I allow it. My doubts sprung from that obscurity. *But*, continues he, *the narrative of sir Thomas More throws great light over all the transactions of the reign of Richard, and over the murder of the two young princes his nephews.* This is begging the very question in dispute. *The magnanimity, the probity and the great sense of that author confirm his testimony; and there is no historian ancient or modern who ought to have more weight.* I must here stop in the middle of this note. In the first place I do not precisely know the meaning of *magnanimity*. It is a pompous but empty word, often employed by another modern historian[3] in lieu of qualities more easily to be defined. When Henry the second had been over-reached, bubbled, baffled, humbled by Becket, and consequently could no longer pass for wife, provident or firm, his panegyrist salves all with the bombast and vague epithet, *magnanimous*: happen what would, his magnanimity was invulnerable. But if *magnanimity* is ridiculous in the mouth of an historian, it is still more absurd when applied *to* an historian. What has *magnanimity* to do with that character? And in what sense does it confirm his testimony? Sir Thomas More's *probi-*

3.   Lord Lyttelton.

ty will prove as little, if I have shown that he has given false evidence. Let Mr. Hume, before he quotes sir Thomas's probity, refute the charge that I have brought against him from facts. A man cannot be a faithful historian if he perverts wilfully, or mistakes facts ignorantly: nor, I should think, would Mr. Hume allow in general that the *probity* of a bigot qualifies him for a sincere historian. Where was sir Thomas's *probity*, or his *great sense*, when he was the dupe of the holy maid of Kent? Mr. Hume too, now become fond of authority, amasses all sir Thomas's great qualities in the various parts of his life, to support a history which More wrote in the very early part of his life, at twenty-eight. I had remarked this; but Mr. Hume did not choose to make the distinction. By a flourish, and tacitly sinking the æra of the composition, he would lead his readers to believe, that the story of Richard the third was written by More in the grave and sedate part of his life, and bequeathed to posterity with all the sanction that the impress of the statesman and martyr could bestow on it. Young Mr. More, under sheriff of London, is the historian Mr. Hume equals with Tacitus, Davila, Thuanus, and all the standard authors of ancient and modern ages! Yet, still the question is not whether sir Thomas lived near the time, but whether his narrative is a competent and probable account. I have questioned his competency, and proved him guilty of ignorant or wilful mistakes. Is it an answer worthy of an able reasoner to tell us, that sir Thomas More lived at or near the time, and that as we have no better account we must believe his? Does Mr. Hume then believe all improbabilities because delivered by cotemporaries,

143

and because he can find no better? Is he under such a necessity, has he such an alacrity of believing, that absurdities are with him preferable to doubting? Must he have an unbroken chain of history reposited in his head, be that history what it will, true or false, marvellous or rational? In theologic controversy divines often repeat, that where you have no better testimony, you must take up with what you have. Does Mr. Hume allow this doctrine? I thought he knew that the accuracy of modern criticism had established two kinds of evidence, the *external* and the *internal*; and that the former, however respectable, is often called in question, when repugnant to the latter. But were Mr. Hume's still newer standard of authority to take place, we should be compelled to believe the origin of Rome, with its Mars, Rhea and the wolf, the marvels of Herodotus, and the fables of ancient Egypt: and in that case I doubt Mr. Hume would be embroiled with Voltaire, the patriarch of modern sceptics, who has called in question a mob of assassinations and poisonings far more credible than those imputed to Richard the third.

Mr. Hume continues: *We may justly regard him* [sir Thomas More] *even as a cotemporary; for though he was but five years old when the two princes were massacred, he lived and was brought up among the chief actors of Richard's reign; and one sees clearly by his recital, which is often very circumstantial, that he received the particularities from ocular witnesses.* This is again equally vague, unfair, and void of argument. Mr. Hume avoids specifying that More received his information from archbishop Morton, who I have proved was the most partial and suspicious authority from whence More could possibly draw his materials; and yet I defy him to show the least probability that More, a retainer of Morton, was likely to converse with any other chief actor of that period. Is it better proof of an author's veracity, that he is very circumstantial? If it is, why has Mr. Hume reposed so little truth in, quoted so little from Wilson, Weldon, Burnet, and others, who give circumstantial accounts of the vices, folly, falsehood and tyranny of four Stuarts? Is there a legend in the monkish writers that is not circumstantial?

We cannot therefore, continues the note, *reject his authority, and it ought to weigh over an hundred light doubts, scruples and objections, for no solid objection has yet been brought against him, nor can he be convicted of any error.* This sentence ex cathedrâ is ridiculous, and fulminated like many bulls against those who do not acknowledge the papal authority. It is easy to say doubts and scruples are light: if they are, they are easily answered. Mr. Hume's infallibility is not more generally recognized, than that of many great men whose authority he himself has set at nought. He will excuse me therefore if I say he asserts only because he cannot answer. Mr. Guthrie and I have shown that sir Thomas More's account of Tirrel is an absolute falsehood. It is proved from record that Tirrel was a great officer of the crown when More represents him as a low creature following the court, but unknown to the king, an intimate of a nameless page, and a fellow ready to be dispatched on any base and sudden assassination. Is this a light doubt, a trifling objection to More's veracity and competence? Sir Thomas adds, that Tirrel, a commissioner for executing the office of high constable in the last reign, and actually master of the horse at the period in question, or, as others say, appointed so within a month, was kept down by Ratcliffe and Catesby, neither of whom ever was Tirrel's equal, and one of whom I have proved was absent at the time.* If these are trifling objections, I invite Mr. Hume to answer them — yes, and to answer sir Thomas More himself, who owns that *there was nothing so plainly and openly proved but that yet men had it ever inwardly suspect*. Mr. Hume, it seems, better informed than sir Thomas himself, knows that sir Thomas was perfectly acquainted with the fact and all the circumstances; and with equal confidence, equally unfounded, declares that *sir Thomas cannot be convicted of any error*!

It is with concern that I am forced to produce the remainder of the first note; nor can I conceive how Mr. Hume could allow himself to make such a misrepresentation of sir Thomas More's evidence in the face of sir Thomas's own words. *It is true*, says Mr. Hume, *that sir Thomas declares that the protector's partisans, in particular doctor Shaw, spread a report of a precontract between Edward the fourth and Elizabeth Lucy, while it appears from records that the parliament pronounced the children of Edward illegitimate, under pretext of a precontract with the lady Eleanor Butler. But*, continues Mr. Hume, *we must observe that no attempt was made to prove either of the contracts; and why should not the protector's flatterers and tools have spread sometimes the one, sometimes the other of those reports?* More quotes both, and treats both as lightly as they deserved. *Mr. Carte thinks it incredible that Richard should have engaged doctor Shaw openly to calumniate the duchess of York his mother, with whom he lived on good terms; but if in reality it is*

146

difficult to believe this, why should not we suppose that the doctor, taking the general matter of his sermon from the protector or his friends, chose himself the particulars, and chose them with very little judgment? The disgrace into which he afterwards fell seems to strengthen his supposition.

I have translated Mr. Hume's words as fairly and faithfully as I am able; and thus I answer them. On the authority of the roll of parliament I accused sir Thomas More of ignorance or falsification in naming Elizabeth Lucy instead of lady Eleanor Butler; and Mr. Hume is forced to admit the evidence, though he would fain avoid the conclusion. This he attempts by urging that sir Thomas mentions both reports. I must own that with all my care I can find no one word in sir Thomas relative to the lady Butler, and would be much obliged to Mr. Hume for pointing out the[4] passage to me. He also speaks of Elizabeth Lucy as a report propagated by the protector's tools and in doctor Shaw's sermon. Unfortunately sir Thomas gives us a *circumstantial* detail of a conversation between king Edward and his mother, in which that princess taxes him with a precontract with Elizabeth Lucy. Did the protector's mother spread those reports? Still farther: "The duchess, says sir Thomas, devised to disturb this marriage [with

4. I have heard that it is mentioned somewhere in the Biographia Britannica, that in a late edition of sir Thomas More's history Eleanor Butler is inserted instead of Elizabeth Lucy. My edition, which is of 1641, has no such correction; and a correction more recent would but prove that sir Thomas More wrote Elizabeth Lucy, and that the grossness of the mistake induced some modern editor to restore the genuine name.

the widow Gray], and rather to help that he should marry one dame Elizabeth Lucy, whom the king had also not long before gotten with child, and openly objected his marriage, as it were in discharge of her conscience, that the king was sure to dame Elizabeth Lucy." Surely, surely, Mr. Hume, this is not a report spread by the protector's tools, but by that very mother whom Richard is accused of aspersing too – and so consistent is your circumstantial oracle, that in one place he ascribes the report to Richard, and in another to the duchess of York. And am I now unfounded in saying that sir Thomas More affirmed deliberately of Elizabeth Lucy what related to Eleanor Butler? What follows is still stronger: "By reason of which words such obstacle was made in the matter, that either the bishops durst not, or the king would not, proceed to the solemnization of this wedding, till these same were clearly purged and the truth well and openly testified. Whereupon dame Elizabeth Lucy was then sent for – and confessed they were never married." "This examination, adds sir Thomas, was solemnly taken." I ask if this proves that doctor Shaw chose the particulars without judgment? And I ask, if what is here said by More is not a wilful or mistaken falsehood? But, says Mr. Hume, no attempt was made to prove either of the contracts. – No! Does not sir Thomas here directly affirm that the bishops refused to marry the king, till the examination was solemnly taken? Which are we to believe, the infallible chancellor, or his determined advocate? Mr. Guthrie goes farther, and, relating the same story of the lady Butler, affirms, as we have seen, that she denied any precontract in open court. So clear is this whole story, after being circumstantially related by sir Thomas More from ocular witnesses! I leave this part to be adjusted as it may by sir Thomas, Mr. Hume and Mr. Guthrie; and proceed to the article of doctor Shaw, of which Mr. Hume is not much happier in his solution.

Mr. Hume, not quite clear whether Mr. Carte is in the right or the wrong, in not believing that the protector aspersed his own mother, though I produced two original papers to prove that he lived in the house with her at the very time of the supposed calumny, and continued on good terms with her, desires us to suppose that doctor Shaw was prompted by the protector in general, but did not choose his materials judiciously. He has guessed that *both* the reports of Lucy and Butler were spread by the protector's agents. This is supposing that a sensible man and artful usurper made choice of very bungling tools, because spreading both reports would have been the surest way of contradicting both reports. But on this point I have better evidence, even that of sir Thomas himself against Mr. Hume, who says, "the protector would that the matter should be *touched aslope craftily." One may see clearly* [to use Mr. Hume's own words] *that sir Thomas is so circumstantial that he must have gathered his materials from the best evidence*; and thence conclude that the protector did not leave the execution of his plot to injudicious tools, but himself adjusted the whole detail of what they should say and do. This is a complete answer to Mr. Hume's supposition, which being raised in opposition to his own evidences, stands on no ground at all: and therefore, when he was reduced to this hypothesis, it is plain that he could not support so silly a story as that of Richard blackening his own mother and setting up a precontract with Elizabeth Lucy: both which I exposed; and which as Mr. Hume cannot defend from the authority of sir Thomas More, without contradicting sir Thomas More, I may fairly presume that I have confuted sir Thomas More, when Mr. Hume himself is forced to give him up, and is forced to deny that he has said what he *has* said so positively and *circumstantially*.

NOTE THE SECOND

If we refute to More the quality of cotemporary relatively to the protectorate of the duke of Gloucester, we cannot deny it to him with regard to the imposture of Perkin. He was then grown a man, and had all the faculties necessary for knowing, examining and deciding on the truth; so that when he assures us that Richard ordered the massacre of the duke of York, he assures us in effect in the clearest manner that Perkin, who assumed his name, was an impostor.

ANSWER

When this note is analysed, I will recommend it for as beautiful an instance of false logic as can be produced. Here is the sum of it: Sir Thomas More was a grown man when Warbeck appeared, and had all the faculties necessary for knowing, examining and deciding on the truth; *therefore* a fact that he relates which passed in his childhood when he was *not* capable of knowing, examining, &c. proves another fact that happened when he was capable of knowing and

150

examining, but which fact he neither related nor examined. Yet even in that circumstance of age Mr. Hume is unfortunate. Sir Thomas was born in 1480; Perkin appeared in 1495, when More was fifteen. Is not that a time of life singularly qualified for knowing, examining and deciding on the truth of a state secret? But perhaps Mr. Hume refers to sir Thomas's age when he composed his history. I have shown that was in his twenty-eighth year, and when he was under-sheriff of London. Was he in a situation then of fathoming all the depths of a mystery which he himself and lord Bacon own had been sedulously involved by Henry the seventh in impenetrable obscurity? Does not sir Thomas confess that he had heard the story of the murder related in many various ways, but gave it from the mouths of those he deemed the most credible witnesses? Was this being in a situation to know, examine and decide peremptorily on so dark a story? Is this assuring us *in the clearest manner* that Richard ordered the murder of his nephews? Does Mr. Hume think that every historian, who is a grown man at or near the time of an event, and who assures us of certain facts, ought to be implicitly received as a faithful reporter? Who stands more strongly in that predicament than doctor Burnet? Who has made a more solemn appeal to heaven for his veracity? I profess I believe the general and by far the greater part of the bishop's history, because I have seen how vain the attempts have been to confute it. — But does Mr. Hume believe so too? If he does, why has he followed him so little? Why are More and Bacon competent witnesses against Richard the third, and Burnet not so against Charles the second?

This note is composed of mere declamation, and assertions unfounded in fact. It contains a pompous panegyric of lord Bacon as a genius of the first water, an excuse for the flattery he has showered on Henry the seventh, and an assumption that it was composed from original papers now lost; with other positions equally arbitrary, which I shall examine presently. I have already observed, that nothing can be weaker than to pretend to establish the credit of an historian on the extent of his understanding. I fear the contrary is more often true; and that the less bright the imagination of an historian, the more he is likely to be exact in his narrative. Many historians are admired for their art, method, style, and shrewdness, on whose fidelity the world does not bestow equal approbation. Perhaps one of the least bright of our historians, Rapin, is more generally esteemed for his veracity than many of his superiors in composition. *But lord Bacon is an upright historian, is not partial to Henry, since it is from him we have received the details of the tyrannic government of that prince. All one can reproach him with is, for not blaming the facts he relates so severely as they deservea.* As the book is in print and common enough, one can scarce conceive how Mr. Hume could give this character of it. If the worst actions are not defended and palliated throughout, if his lordship's tacit disapprobation of them may be conjectured, as it is true it sometimes may, still so timidly is it insinuated, so cautiously enveloped, that he seems to have hoped the learned prince [James the first] under whose auspices the work was composed, would not have sagacity enough to pentrate his real sentiments. But I will recur to the book itself. In the dedication to prince Charles, lord Bacon professes *that he has endeavoured to do honour to the memory of that king*, [Henry the seventh] and the history takes care to keep the promise made by the dedication. *Besides*, continues the dedication, *the times deserve it, for he was a wise man and an excellent king*. This was the text, and we find it amply handled in the same style. I shall select a few instances, and will leave the reader to judge whether lord Bacon is solely reproachable with not having treated Henry's tyranny with due rigour, as Mr. Hume asserts; or whether, as I pretend, he has not exalted some of his worst actions into matter of panegyric: and under this head I shall forbear recapitulating the instances I have already quoted in the Historic Doubts.

Henry procured the Star-chamber, which before subsisted by the common law, to be confirmed in certain cases by act of parliament. This court, says lord Bacon, is one of the sagest and noblest institutions of this kingdom.

Recounting the reasons that moved Henry to put to death sir William Stanley, the brother of his own mother's husband, lord Bacon reckons those that were predominant in the king's nature and mind, as, *Stanley's overmerit and the glimmering of a confiscation, for he was the richest subject for value in the kingdom* — and after assigning these base and scandalous motives, he adds these words: *after some six weeks distance of time, which the king did honourably interpose, both to give time to his brother's intercession and to show to the world that he had a conflict with himself what to do, Stanley was arraigned, condemned and beheaded*. This *honourable* hypocrisy is something more

153

methinks than not treating Henry with proper severity. And these sordid motives weighed to get rid of a man, whom lord Bacon impiously compares to Jesus Christ, *as having had the benefit at once to save and crown.* p. 135.

On the inhuman murder of the young and simple earl of Warwick the noble historian is as indulgent as possible, and rather treats it as an act of political wisdom. "It happened opportunely, says he, that while the king was meditating that young prince's death, another counterfeit started up to represent the danger to the king's estate, and thereby to colour the king's severity that followed. And to shift the envy of so foul a deed from himself, the king thought good to transport it out of the land, and to lay it upon his new ally the king of Spain: for these two kings understanding one another at half a word, Ferdinand refused to give his daughter to prince Arthur, while the earl of Warwick was alive." Is it possible to palliate a shocking murder by smoother terms? And did not the sage Henry by this infamous intrigue avow that the earl of Warwick had the best title to the crown, from the illegitimacy of Henry's own queen and her sisters? In truth, among the instances of his boasted wisdom, there is scarce one in which he did not prove the dupe of his own duplicity, and of the superior cunning of others. But I should tire the reader and myself with recapitulating what the whole book demonstrates, that it is the panegyric of a knavish tyrant, and in no light deserves the rank to which Mr. Hume would prefer it. I will only observe farther, that in the end he calls him *the Solomon of England, and a wonder for wise men*, and talks of the piety, charity, morality, justice and lenity, of a tyrant who plundered his people by every act of extortion, shed innocent blood from jealousy, wrenched the laws to serve his purposes, and died mocking God by commanding his son to put to death the earl of Suffolk whom he had sworn himself to save.

Mr. Hume's next assertion in this note is, that lord Bacon composed his history from authentic papers now lost; and therefore ought always to be cited as an original writer. Lord Bacon no where pretends to have seen any such papers: it is a mere ipse dixit of Mr. Hume, who being the sole finder of those papers was certainly at liberty to lose them again if he pleased. Lord Bacon's history was rather composed like Xenophon's Cyrus, for a model to princes, than as a strict and faithful narrative. Livy, Josephus, Eusebius, and even Varillas, might by Mr. Hume's argument be equally entitled to universal credit. The first founded all his fables of the early ages of Rome on writers long since perished: and the three others pretended to have consulted authentic monuments and papers in the composition of their several works, and yet, though on that foot original writers, are now treated by all men of sense as fabulous romancers. But Mr. Hume takes great care to forget that the truth of history does not depend solely on the originality of an author. A thousand circumstances must concur to establish his credit. A cotemporary, if not an actor, is seldom well informed, and the first histories we have are generally the least true. Time brings greater evidence to light, and dissipates the clouds of party, partiality, and mistake. Why else has Mr. Hume taken the trouble of recomposing what has been so often written?

I will conclude my remarks on this note with exemplifying two more round assertions in it, as little founded as the preceding. In lord Bacon's time, says Mr. Hume, it was no longer any body's interest to blacken Richard. I have stated, and I thought clearly, that it was as unsafe in king James's time, as in king Henry's, to assert the bastardy of the children of Edward the fourth. James the first claimed from the eldest daughter of Henry and Elizabeth. In the very last years of queen Elizabeth, not twenty-five years before lord Bacon wrote his history, various claims to the crown had been set forth in opposition to that of James. The earls of Huntingdon, Derby, and others, were descended from different branches of the royal stock, whose titles were preferable to those of Henry, who had in reality no title at all, and even of his wife Elizabeth, if her mother's was not a lawful marriage. I am not surprised that Mr. Hume should overlook my arguments, but he will not wonder if I think them preferable to his assertions founded on no argument at all, and contrary to fact.

But the most strange assertion of all is, Mr. Hume's pretending, contrary to the evidence of his own eyes, that lord Bacon had no doubt of Perkin being an impostor. I have stated in the Historic Doubts various expressions of lord Bacon, which evince, that whatever pains he took to persuade others, he was by no means convinced himself. The immunity of Lambert Simnel, *which was no finall argument that there was some secret in it; the king's manner of muffling the story, which has left it almost a mystery to this day;* his owning *that the king did himself no good* by the publication of the narrative — these and twenty

other expressions must convince us that lord
Bacon was far from having any inward conviction that Perkin was not the true duke of York;
and that, if my doubts are light and trifling,
Mr. Hume's assertions are so overloaded with
false weight, that they will sink themselves in
the mind of every impartial reader.

But without guessing at the depths of so
insincere a mind as lord Bacon's, here is positive
proof that he did not believe the story as he
related it. he has composed a new confession for
Perkin, different from and irreconcileable with
that published by king Henry. This I stated
before. Mr. Hume could not answer it, and
consequently overlooked it – at the expence of
his accuracy. I offer it to him once more thus:
Lord Bacon could not compose a new confession
for Perkin, without thinking that that given out
by Henry was a fiction; and certainly not
without knowing that what he himself composed in lieu of it, was so. Was it from these
two impostures that lord Bacon believed Perkin
was an impostor?

NOTE THE FOURTH

But if we demand, says Mr. Hume, cotemporary evidence, the strongest and least suspicious are ready with their testimony. He then
musters a long list of the queen and first persons
and families, who, says he, were so persuaded of
the murder of the two princes, that they addres-
sed themselves to the earl of Richmond, the
mortal enemy of their family and party.* Here
let us pause a moment. – Mr. Hume formerly,
making use of the same argument, was so
unlucky as to mistake Lancastrians for Yorkists.

Corrected now, though without owning his mistake, he has invented a new muster-roll of names, still without offering the least authority to inform us from whence he took them. He has dubbed them all Yorkists at once. That they all submitted afterwards to the usurper Henry, I do not doubt, esepcially after he had married the heiress of York. For such of them as joined to invite Richmond over, their belief or disbelief of the murder proves just nothing at all, but that they deserted the right heirs of the crown, and entered into a conspiracy to place it on the head of a bastard branch. Let Richard be what he would, his usurpation could give no title to Henry. If the princes were dead and their sisters legitimate, the latter were the next heirs. There were also many other princes and princesses living of the house of York. As it appeared afterwards that the counties in which the chief interest of that family lay, maintained their affection and attachment to that house, Mr. Hume will excuse me if I do not believe from his fictitious roll of names that the party of York did concur in general in the invitation to Henry; and though he lays great stress on illustrious names, whoever calls to mind the factions of that time and their frequent changes from interested views, and whoever has seen any thing of factions at all, will not form his opinion of a cause from the behaviour of the most illustrious persons on either side. Much less will he pay regard to a second edition of names, supported, according to Mr. Hume's method, by no authority.

But, as if he was sensible of the weakness of his argument, he endeavours to prop the question he has begged, by asking the most wonderful question that I suppose was ever asked since the days of the schoolmen. They indeed used to enquire how things would have been, if they had been very different from what they were; as how Adam and Eve would have begotten children, if they had both been women? Our new Tostatus proposes the following quære in support of his imaginary host of Yorkists: *Is there one*, says he, *of these persons, who in writing the memoirs of their own time would not have assured us that Richard murdered his nephews?* − In truth, I have not such intuition into what never existed, as to know how a nothing would be, if it had ever been. Would Mr. Hume allow me that Charles the first was a tyrant and murderer, because I should assert that Bradshaw, Ireton, and Hugh Peters, who never did write his history, would have represented him as such, if they ever had written his history? How difficult is it to establish the received history of Richard, when so able a man as Mr. Hume is reduced to suppose that it would be confirmed by the writings of his bitterest enemies, if those enemies had given any account of him! A man less bright than Mr Hume would suspect that such non-existent hypothetical authors would have been partial. His Promethean sagacity, after creating the persons, has discovered not only what they would have written, but argues from this posthumous kind of non-entities. This is a fair and fruitful addition to the stores of disputation: its latitude is unbounded: it may serve alike the cause of truth and falsehood, and does equal honour to the ingenious gentleman who invented this sort of argument, and to his friend the Swiss reviewer, who was only dazzled by my old-fashioned arguments, but was convinced by the luminous force and solidity of this new method of induction.

Is built on Richard's supposed intention of marrying his niece.* Unluckily it proves nothing at all. If the young duke of York escaped, Richard certainly did not know whether he was living or dead. If Richard designed to marry his niece, it was to prevent her espousing Richmond. These roundabout ways of supposing the murder, are the shifts of one that cannot prove the imposture of Perkin. Prove that, and I will not dispute the murder. It is the strong evidence in favour of his being the true duke of York that invalidates the murder. Mr. Hume had rather do any thing than discuss that evidence. He flies from it to presumptions, fantastic bead-rolls of names, unwritten memoirs, and non-repeals of acts of parliament. With him, the *not* repealing an act of parliament is a proof that there was no ground for making it. By the same kind of logic, a repeal ought to corroborate an act of parliament.

NOTE THE SIXTH

In a string of propositions it is usual to increase the strength of the argument. Mr. Hume has inverted this method. The farther he advances, the weaker his reasons, till he concludes with one that precedes the faculty of reasoning, and is calculated only for the nursery. In the note before me, after endeavouring from historians and actors to establish the murder, he has recourse to the reports spread in foreign nations. Let Mr. Hume, if he can, refute my arguments in favour of Perkin Warbeck; I willingly resign to him the sudden impression spread in France by Richard's enemies, and the recent and more mature judgment of the Swiss reviewer. Let me however observe, that the emperor of China refused to receive an embassy from a great princess on much the same plea that Charles the eighth urged against Richard's embassadors. Would Mr. Hume, his friends messieurs Dalembert and Diderot, and Voltaire, who have celebrated the tolerating and legislative spirit of that heroine, allow that the Chinese monarch's ill-breeding was a proof that the most atrocious reports were well-founded?

NOTE THE SEVENTH

Still advancing like a lively crab in retrograde argumentation, Mr. Hume next presents us with every body's oration. Every body, says he, argued thus and thus: and then, like a good christian, sums up this harangue with a quotation from scripture. "Richard, says he, could not plead like Cain, Am I the keeper of my nephews?" I am rejoiced that saint Cain is admitted into Mr. Hume's rubric. "Richard, continues he, might have answered the accusation by producing his nephews." – What! if one or both had escaped, and were not in his power? Thus Mr. Hume supposes the very point to be proved, and wonders it is disputed, after he has taken it for granted.* I have so good an opinion of his sagacity, that if he had *not* taken it for granted *before* he wrote his history, I am persuaded he would not believe it now. There is a good deal of difference in the kind of belief

161

which a man entertains *before* he has treated a subject, and *after*.

NOTE THE EIGHTH

Is built on the evidence of Tirrel, which I have examined distinctly in my Doubts, and there challenged Mr. Hume to show how it was possible for Perkin to agree in his narrative with Tirrel and Dighton, unless he was the true duke of York; supposing Tirrel made the confession alleged, which I have shown to be most improbable. If Tirrel did *not* make that confession, there is no evidence of the murder, but the declaration of Dighton, who, says lord Bacon, *spake best for the king*, and whose testimony is invalidated by every rule of evidence. I own there is less trouble in repeating the words *Tirrel* and *Dighton*, than in answering those arguments – and Mr. Hume has chosen the easier part. Indeed I do not conceive why my book was worth answering, and not my arguments.

NOTE THE NINTH

If the duke of York had escaped, says Mr. Hume, *the queen his mother, the duchess of Burgundy, and all those attached to his family would have been made acquainted with it*. I agree with him on the two former, not at all on the rest. It was too important a secret to be confided to many. The illustrious partisans of that or any party were not, I doubt, so immaculate as to deserve a trust of such consequence. The queen and duchess probably were informed: and it is odd to hear Mr. Hume complaining that the secret was not trusted to the duchess, when she was the

162

principal supporter of Perkin. Mr. Hume is surprised that she was not let into the secret; and presently will reject her own declaration that she knew him for her nephew. Henry's treatment of the queen dowager, and her close imprisonment with prohibition of all access, is a stronger presumption of her being privy to that fatal secret, than any Mr. Hume can bring to show that she did not know it.

NOTE THE TENTH

Our total ignorance of those who assisted the duke of York in his escape is sufficient proof of the imposture of Perkin. If Perkin had obtained the crown, this would be something of an argument. Did not the pretender escape from Scotland, because Mr. Hume does not *know* who assisted him?

NOTE THE ELEVENTH

Perkin's narrative is void of all probability. – I know it. Lord Bacon thought so, and composed a new one for him. What consequence ought to be drawn thence? Why, that we have not his genuine narrative, but such as were composed for him by Henry the seventh and the Lancastrian historians. Mr. Hume is as unhappy in his conclusions as in his assertions.

NOTE THE TWELFTH

Perkin made an entire confession of his imposture, and read it three times. We do not find the least insinuation that it was drawn from him by torture; and when he made it the last time, he had certainly nothing to fear.

ANSWER

It would be highly unreasonable in me to take offence at Mr. Hume's forgetting all my arguments, and all the answers which I have already given to his, [for indeed he does little more than repeat what he had said before] when he takes the liberty of contradicting a person who ought to have much greater weight with him, I mean himself. In his notes on his own history he informs us, that Perkin's confession was supposed [though he questions it] to be wrung from him by torture. He now positively asserts that we do not find the least insinuation of such force being employed. This is asserting and denying to some purpose. With regard to the confession, he does not inform us to which he adheres, to Henry's or Bacon's. No matter: we cannot believe both, and both give us cause to believe neither. Henry's was rejected by the infallible Bacon, and his own substitution of another destroys that too. That Perkin had nothing farther to fear, is asserted with as little foundation. Have we never heard in arbitrary governments [such was that of England then] of men submitting on imposed conditions to a milder death, to avoid one more cruel? Who knows whether Perkin [supposing he made a confession, which is most improbable] read it in an audible voice; or whether Henry's tools and sheriffs and guards did not disperse a paper after his death, and affirm he had delivered it to them? Were the histories of those times written *circumstantially as they are now? Indeed, which history of that time was written at the time? Sir Thomas More does not go so low: lord Bacon and the rest wrote many years afterwards.*

NOTE THE THIRTEENTH

If Henry had not been convinced that Perkin was a ridiculous impostor, he would not have let him live an hour after he had got him in his power. The manner in which he treated the innocent earl of Warwick gives great force to this argument.

ANSWER

I do not presume to trouble Mr. Hume or any body else with looking over the detail I have given of Henry's anxiety and suspicions on Perkin's account; and of the difference of his behaviour towards him and Lambert Simnel, who was a ridiculous impostor, and whom Henry treated accordingly. But if Mr. Hume does not *purposely* choose to confound this conduct on two very different subjects, I would beg him to peruse once more his infallible Bacon, and see whether Henry thought that Perkin was an object of contempt and ridicule.

The latter part of the note is as extraordinary an oversight [I will call it no more] as the former. "Had Henry been convinced that Perkin was the true duke of York, he would not have let him live an hour, but would have treated him as he did the young earl of Warwick." Henry had reigned at least nine years before Perkin appeared. The earl of Warwick was all that time in Henry's power, and it was at least two years before the latter was put to death. Perkin was not in Henry's hands as many *months*, as Warwick had been *years*, before Henry caused him to be executed. Does not Mr. Hume's argument contract, as he boasts, great force from this happy illustration?

Enter the duchess of Burgundy on the other side of the question. Just now Mr. Hume argued from her knowing nothing of her nephew; now it seems she knew too much. Like Hudibras, Mr. Hume can take up his arms, dispute,

"Confute, change sides, and still confute himself back again."

She had adopted Simnel, and therefore was not to be credited about Perkin. Mr Hume demands that she should be acquainted with the fate of her nephew; she tells you she is. — Therefore what? Therefore do not believe her. — But I will rest contented with Mr. Hume's contradicting himself, as he has done in so many instances, and shall leave the reader to judge from what I have said in the Doubts, whether Henry or Margaret set up an imposture?

But I cannot so easily abandon Mr. Carte to the attacks of that powerful *whig*-champion, Mr. Hume, who has no mercy on a poor dead man, only because he was attached to that nonsensical tenet *hereditary right*. *Mr. Carte*, says he, to blacken Henry the seventh for having no hereditary right, suppressed entirely the important fact of the duchess supporting Simnel.* Is it then an irremissible crime in an historian to suppress any material fact? I do not know, nor can I take the trouble now to examine whether Mr. Carte has suppressed the negotiations between Charles the first and the pope's nuncio, so unanswerably proved upon him by the exact Mrs. Macaulay. I myself have declared that it was natural for Charles to treat with Roman catholic subjects against protestant subjects who endeavoured to dethrone him. But what becomes of his protestant piety, his martyrdom, his sincerity? Look at the concessions he made on every capital point, and the oaths he swore to conceal them. If Mr. Carte has suppressed this enormous treaty, and has still represented Charles in an amiable light, I shall indeed allow that he has stifled an important fact, and will abandon him to my whig friend — but an historian may omit less material circumstances, and not deserve the same censure. For instance: Burnet assures us that sir Edmundbury Godfrey told him that he expected to be knocked on the head. This circumstance is entirely omitted by a late masterly historian, though very material with regard to the murder that ensued: but it did not suit the hypothesis of Godfrey's murdering himself. *Vide Hume's Reign of Charles II.*

I will not wander from my subject to lay open many other errors and omissions in the history I have here quoted, though I could loosen its artful texture in variety of places with far greater facility than I have unravelled the story of Richard the third. I admire the ingenious fabric with all its want of symmetry, and in spite of the conflict with which it is ever at war with itself, by endeavouring to separate those hearty friends the prerogative and the church, and by fruitlessly trying to exalt the former and decry the latter; an attempt that tenders the whole work one beautiful contradiction.

NOTE THE FIFTEENTH

No proofs, says Mr. Hume, *were produced at the*

time, of Perkin's being the true duke of York. How
does he know? When so much accumulative
evidence in his favour, after all the labours of
Henry and his partisans to destroy it, yet
remains, sure the probability is, that still greater appeared at the time. From what Henry
forged, we may guess at what he suppressed.
We have none but Lancastrian historians: the
queen was shut up, and, by lord Bacon's own
confession, every thing so muffled by Henry,
that it staggered every body. Mr. Hume, cut-
ting the Gordian knot which he could not
untie, asserts with the tone of an Alexander,
that all Perkin's answers might have been easily
suggested to him by the duchess of Burgundy,
by Frion, and by whoever had lived in the court
at that time. I have shown to demonstration by
dates, which Mr. Hume swallows as if they were
expletives, that the duchess did *not* live in the
court at any part of the time; and any man's
common sense, but Mr. Hume's, will tell him,
that it is absolutely impossible to instruct a
stranger so thoroughly in all the passages of a
court, that he would not be detected in an
hour's time. If my book is not a heap of
absurdities, there is no part of it less liable to be
contested than the passages in which I have
stated the true and obvious method of detecting
such an impostor, if he was one. I have shown
that the omission of such satisfaction, and the
substitution of the most absurd assertions, create the strongest objections against Henry. If I
have talked nonsense, it would be charity in Mr.
Hume to set me right. He knows the deference I
have for his understanding, and no doubt he, if
he pleased, could convince me that Henry's
conduct was clear, rational, and liable to no

misrepresentation: that lord Bacon's account of his ambiguity is false, and yet that lord Bacon's account ought to be implicitly relied on. Mr. Hume could certainly disprove all that I have said, and prove all that he has said himself, though as yet he has done neither. Nay, I am persuaded he could do what is still more difficult, since his eloquence has worked that miracle both on himself and his friend the reviewer, convince me by weak arguments and groundless assertions, that the authority of great names is preferable to solid reasons; and that repeating arguments that have been confuted, gives them new force. Women and drunken men make use of that kind of oratory; and perhaps Mr. Hume's example may give new weight to the practice.

The note concludes with confessing that many persons of distinction were *at first* deceived by Perkin, which he ascribes to the enthusiasm of the nation in favour of the house of York. – I thought that all the illustrious Yorkists, according to Mr. Hume's catalogue of them, knew for certainty that the children were murdered. How came they to unknow it again? *But*, says he, *many were at first deceived*. Would not one think that that persuasion had been momentary? Does Mr. Hume forget, or with the art of a disputant did he slip in the words *at first* to make his reader forget, that four or five knights of the garter and privy-counsellors to Henry were convinced Perkin was king Edward's son, and died in that persuasion? Does such attestation of their belief accord with Mr. Hume's assertion in the beginning of the note, that *no proofs* were produced at the time, of Perkin being the true duke of York? This manner of stating a fact and evading the just conclusion, I call owning truth without allowing it: it is endeavouring to delude with a clear conscience. The poor reviewer fell into the snare — I do not believe any body else will.

NOTE THE SIXTEENTH

The last note, which establishes the murder on the authority of the bones found in the Tower, is the only note to which I shall not presume to give an answer. Untouched let it subsist to the comfort and edification of all the good women who visit the tombs in Westminster-abbey! May those bones remain an equal proof of the crimes of Richard, and of the catholic credulity of Mr. Hume and the reviewer! In those pious lands where all the evidence of a miracle depends on showing the rotten remains of those to whom, or the spot on which it happened, such faith is often found. — In truth, I did not expect it would make its appearance in the form of an argument — but since Mr. Hume is reduced to reason from relics, he will excuse me if I leave him at the door of the sanctuary, and am still unbeliever enough to think that those bones so enshrined are no more a proof of the guilt of Richard, than they are of the piety of Charles the second.*

I have thus replied to Mr. Hume's remarks; an attention certainly due to whatever falls from so superior a writer. I am not entitled to the same observance from him; nor would the public excuse me, if he wasted some of those moments in answering my objections, which he can employ so much better for their instruction and amusement. In truth, they expect greater things from him. As he has been admitted into the penetralia of the Benedictine college at Paris, and has explored the authentic secrets of the two last Stuarts, the public is impatient for the detail of those mysteries, of which he has already given them a hint: nor can the appetite which *he* has raised be satisfied with a meagre note. He has another and still greater achievement to perform, which can never be executed by so masterly a hand, and which the world eagerly demands from his; a work more worthy of his genius, than any on which it has yet been exercised. As Mr. Hume's talent certainly veers to panegyric rather than satire, it must be a grateful satisfaction to so generous a mind to bestow deserved encomiums, instead of softening defects and excesses. The reign of king William, who expelled the tyrants of Britain and tools of France, will shine with all its lustre when treated by a philosopher and patriot, who prefers the rights, the liberty, the happiness of mankind, to the selfish politics of narrow-minded kings, and to the base adulation of venal courts. In Mr. Hume's page we shall read with pleasure the establishment and extent of our invaluable constitution, as immoveably founded on the revolution – and the excellent doctor Robertson will not remain the first of historians, who, above the little prejudices of country, party, and profession, has dared to speak of the natural rights of mankind with just boldness, and has traced the progress of despotism in such glorious glowing colours, as must warn the few free nations yet remaining on earth to watch the silent craft and undermining policy of princes and statesmen.

Having now dispatched all the straws that

have been thrown in my way, may I be allowed to add to what I have formerly said, some additional confirmations of my opinion?

A very sensible gentleman, whose name I will not mix with Guthrie's and reviewers, on reading my book, sent me a small volume of notes that he had drawn up forty years ago, in which I was flattered to find very many of my own remarks, and others of great weight, which I should be proud to be at liberty to publish.* This is a proof that my opinion is not singular. Indeed, Rapin, Carte, and others, had seen the objection that ought to be made to Lancastrian historians. Mr. Hume calls Carte's doubts whimsical; and mine, light scruples. With submission, they are not whimsical or light scruples, which so profound a reasoner as Mr. Hume can answer no better.

With regard to the person of Richard, the earl of Shaftsbury was so good as to inform me, that his ancestor the lady Ashley, who lived to a great age, had conversed with lady Desmond, and gave from her the same account that I have given, with this strong addition, that Perkin Warbeck was remarkably like Edward the fourth. And to prove that the print I have exhibited of Richard and his queen, which the late bishop of Carlisle believed was taken from a window in the priory of Little Malvern [destroyed by a storm some years ago], was not a fantastic picture of imagination, I shall here present the reader with two more portraits of Richard and his queen, almost minutely corresponding with Vertue's drawing, and taken from the best and most unquestionable authority. The earl of Sandwich, on reading my Doubts, obligingly acquainted me that the duke of

Manchester was possessed of a most curious and original roll, containing the list, portraits and descent of all the earls of Warwick, drawn by John Rous himself, the antiquary. This singular manuscript his grace, at my desire, was so good as to lend me; and with his permission I caused ten of the last and most curious portraits to be traced off, and here present them to the the public faithfully and exactly engraven.*

The roll is on parchment, and is seven yards and a half long; perfectly preserved within, but by handling damaged on the outside, on which have been painted many coats of arms.

The list begins with Guthalmus, and contains the effigies of several imaginary saints and heroes, many kings of England, and the portrait of Richard the third, with whom it concludes, twice; all neatly tricked, and the habits of the most distant ages, as well as of the succeeding, judiciously observed. On the outside is written

"This roll was laburd and finished by master John Rows of Warwick."

But perhaps the most curious part of this curiosity is the following inscription under Richard, which shows that, whatever Rous chose to say of him in compliment to Henry the seventh, he gave a very different account of him in his roll, which he left to posterity, as a monument of the earls and town to which he was so much attached. Here is the inscription as it was written by Rous's own hand:

"The moost mighty prince Richard by the grace of God kynge of Ynglond and of Fraunce and lord of Irelond, by verey matrymony, wtowt dyscontynewance or any defylynge yn the

173

lawe, by eyre male lineally dyscendyng fro kynge Harre the second, all avaryce set asyde, rewled his subjettyrs in hys realme ful comendabylly, puneshynge offenders of hys lawes, specyally extorcioners and oppressers of his comyns, and cheryshynge tho yat were vertuos, by the whyche dyscrete guydynge he gat gret thank of God and love of all hys subjettys ryche and pore, and gret lawd of the people of all othyr landys abowt hym."*

Mr. Hume declares his affection to cotemporary and original authors. I beseech him to produce one more genuine, more uncastrated, less interpolated than this record, existing in the very hand writing of the author. Let him try it by his rules of originality, and compare it with the testimonies of More and Bacon. He will tell me, perhaps, that Rous in his history has said the very reverse. True, in a book dedicated to Richard's rival and successor. Lay Richard for a moment out of the question, and let Mr. Hume tell me on any indifferent point which evidence he would prefer. Would he believe Rous flattering Henry to his face; or Rous in his cell delivering his opinion of a dead king? for it is evident that in the inscription Rous speaks of Richard as one that *had* ruled.*

I do not doubt but the able critics with whom I have been engaged, would treat my conjecture as light and whimsical, if I said I believed [and yet I must avow I do believe] that the remarkable and by no means indifferent words *by very matrimony without discontinuance or any defiling in the law, by heir male lineally descending*, allude to the bigamy of Edward the fourth and the illegitimacy of his children. I firmly believe too that the subsequent words *all avarice set aside,*

174

punishing offenders of his laws, especially extortioners and oppressors of his commons, were a tacit satire on the usurer his successor. I have at least produced here much better authority in vindication of Richard than Mr. Hume can bring against him; for he cannot reject the testimony of Rous, without giving up those criterions of truth, which he has established as demanding our assent and trust.

I said in my Doubts, that I was ready to yield to better reasons than my own; but I did not say I would yield to worse. Still less was I ever inclined to accept of great names instead of any reasons at all. If mere authority would do, Mr. Hume would have as much weight with me as Bacon or More: but great men without their great sense strike me with no more awe than their monuments, which only exhibit their titles and cover their dust. We shed a tear over their ashes and their weaknesses, but bestow our tribute of praise on those excellencies alone which touch the heart or convince the understanding.

May 10, 1769

FINIS

P.S. Since the above notes were written, I have found two passages, that evidently show how vague and uncertain the reports relating to the death of Edward the fifth and his brother were even in the life-time of sir Thomas More. From that very scarce book called The Pastyme of the People, and better known by the title of Rastell's Chronicle, in the possession of Mr.

John Ratcliffe of Rotherhithe, I transcribed verbatim the following paragraphs:

"But of the maner of the dethe of this yonge kynge and of his brother, there were dyvers opinyons. But the most comyn opinyon was that they were smoldery'd betwene two fether-beddes, and that in the doynge the yonger brother escaped from under the fetherbeddes, and crept under the bedstede, and there lay naked awhyle, tyll that they had smoldery'd the yonge kyng, so that he was surely dede. And aftery^t. one of them toke his brother from under the bedstede and hylde his face downe to the grounde with his one hande, and with the other hande cut his throte holle a sonder with a dagger. It is a mervayle that any man coude have so harde a harte to do so cruell a dede, save onely that necessyte compelled them, for they were so charged by the duke the protectour, that if they shewed nat to hym the bodyes of bothe those chylderne dede on the morowe after they were so comaunded, that than they them-selfe shulde be put to dethe. Wherefore they that were comaunded to do it were compelled to fulfyll the protectour's wyll. And after that the bodyes of these II chylderne as the opinyon ranne were bothe closed in a great hevy cheste, and by the meanes of one that was secrete with the protectour, they were put in a shyppe goynge to Flaunders; and whan the shyppe was in the blacke depes this man threwe bothe those dede bodyes so closed in the cheste over the hatches into the see, and yet none of the maryners nor none in the shyppe, save onely the sayd man, wyst what thynge it was that was there so inclosed; which sayenge dyvers men conjectured to be trewe, because that the bones

176

of the sayd chylderne coude never be founde buryed nother in the Towre nor in no other place."

"Another opinyon there is that they whiche had the charge to put them to dethe caused one to cry so sodaynly treason, treason, wherewith the chylderne beynge aferde, desyred to knowe what was best for them to do. And than they bad them hyde themselfe in a great cheste that no man shulde fynde them, and if any body came into the chambre, they wolde say they were nat there. And accordynge as they counsellyd them, they crepte bothe into the cheste, which anone after they locked. And than anone they buryed that cheste in a great pytte under a steyre, which cheste was after caste into the blacke depes, as is before sayd."

I shall pass over the absurdities of both the foregoing accounts; but how will they strike us, when we find from Ames's Typographical Antiquities, p. 147, that this book was printed in 1529, the twenty-first year of Henry the eighth, and from p. 141, that Rastell the compiler and printer married sir Thomas More's own sister? If sir Thomas, as Mr. Hume pretends, was so intimate with the chief persons of Richard's court or reign, how came he to suffer his brother-in-law to pass such senseless stuff on the public, in a work no doubt submitted to his inspection? for Rastell was not only his relation but printer, his very next publication being a dialogue written by More and printed in the same year with the Chronicle. Nor did sir Thomas pick up the materials for his own history after the appearance of Rastell's Chronicle, which was published but six years before sir Thomas's death, when the persons from whom he gained his intelligence must have been dead likewise. But do not sir Thomas's own words betray, not only doubts in his own breast, but thorough proof of the uncertainty of all the incidents relative to the murder? He tells us, that he does not relate the murder in every way he had heard it, but according to the most probable account he could collect from the most creditable witnesses. And I will ask one or two more questions, which I defy Mr. Hume or any man living to answer in a rational manner. If Dighton and Tirrel confessed the murder in the reign of Henry the seventh, how could even the outlines be a secret and uncertain in the reign of Henry the eighth? Is it credible that they owned the fact, and concealed every one of the circumstances? If they related those circumstances, without which their confession could gain no manner of belief, could sir Thomas More, chancellor to Henry the eighth, and educated in the house of the prime minister to Henry the seventh, be ignorant of what it was so much the interest of cardinal Morton to tell, and of Henry the seventh to have known and ascertained? A king and his brother are murdered (according to Henry, More, Bacon, Hume, Guthrie, and the mob), a great officer of the crown and a low groom confess themselves principals in the guilt, the first is executed, the latter suffered to live, to disperse the tale. Neither of them give the least account *how* they committed the fact; or, if they did, no man living from the prime minister to the compiler of the Chronicle could get *certain* intelligence of what they confessed, though it is impossible to assign any other reason for the impunity of Dighton, but the intention of his spreading and authenticating the story. If therefore the confessions said to be made by Tirrel and Dighton are irreconcileable to every standard by which we can judge of evidence, no evidence of the murder exists. If the attestations produced by Henry, More, and Bacon, who indubitably furnished the best they could, are inconsistent and improbable, the identity of Perkin Warbeck and the duke of York remains unshaken, Mr. Hume himself allowing and bending all the force of his argument to prove, that the strong evidence against Perkin is the certainty of the murder. If, on the contrary, the authority of historians is sufficient to pass such stuff on our credulity, I must avow I cannot see what criterion there is in human reason by which we may distinguish between truth and the most clumsy and incoherent legends.

August 6, 1769

A REPLY
TO THE OBSERVATIONS
OF THE REV. DR. MILLES,

Dean of Exeter, and President of the Society of Antiquaries

ON THE WARDROBE ACCOUNT OF 1483, &c

Printed at the End of Archæologia, or Miscellaneous Tracts relating to Antiquity. Published by the Society of Antiquaries of London, 1770.

La prévention se laisse vaincre insensiblement; malheur à qui l'attaque le premier; il en essuye toute l'opiniàtreté & tout l'emportement, mais de jour en jour elle s'assoiblit; et il ne faut que continuerde lapresser pour la détruire. – *La Motte, Réflexions sur la critique*, vol. iii. p. 248.

Notwithstanding the encouragement of so able and amiable a critic as monsieur la Motte, I had certainly no inclination to pursue the controversy relative to Richard III. It is a subject of no consequence; I expressed my doubts on it; I concluded doubting; and should never have believed that I had had much success in clearing away a considerable part of the rubbish with which the story had been loaded, if my answers had not proved that, with all their prejudice in favour of antiquated nonsense, they could not restore it to its place. It is still very indifferent to me how much they choose to believe without reason and contrary to common sense. It is even diverting to see what straws they catch at, when their legend is sinking. One of them believes all the crimes charged on Richard, because he himself had confuted many of them, and I had taken no notice of it. *Vide the Critical Review.* Another, because the king's servants may mean his royal brothers. *Vide the London Chronicle.* And a third, because, if some of Richard's enemies, who never did write his history, had written his history, he supposes they would have given the same absurd account of him.* We shall see presently that the last answerer believes all the guilt of Richard for two reasons that do not yield in weight to any of the three former. To convince such understandings by argument, let monsieur la Motte say what he will, I firmly believe impossible: nor do I care enough for Richard the third to desire it. All I propose is, to show that they have not answered my arguments, and after that, Credat Judæus Apella.

That I was at first treated, in the words of the passage above, with *emportement*, was true – and was comical. That I am still to encounter obstinacy, is no less true – I cannot say comical too, because I am sorry when a worthy person lets the public see that his abilities are not so great as his virtues. I have so great a regard for the reverend president of our society, that I beg he will understand, if I smile at his efforts, that I preserve all due regard for his person and merit.

I was told last winter, that our venerable president had read at the society an answer to my Historic Doubts. As I have long ceased attending public societies, as well as quitted my seat in parliament, it is not extraordinary that I was not present to undergo that humiliation at the feet of Gamaliel. In truth, I enquired little after his confutation, as the reverend person above a year before had acquainted me with his

181

objections, and they had appeared to me so trifling, that I had little curiosity to learn more of them. However, I now-and-then heard that some persons, who had wished my doubts could be answered, and who would have been more glad if they had been able to answer them themselves, affected to pronounce the dean's work a full confutation of my book. At last I read in the newspapers that the reverend president himself had presented the memoires of our society to his majesty. – I sent for the book; expecting to see at least some attempt towards answering the chain of arguments by which I had shown the probability of Perkin Warbeck being the true duke of York. Some endeavours I thought must be made to reconcile the contradictory accounts of Henry the seventh and lord Bacon; and as I had rested the whole of what I had said on the impossibility of Perkin's knowing what passed in the Tower, unless he had been the real duke of York, I looked eagerly for an answer to that challenge – and what did I find? Not a word on Perkin Warbeck, but that entire argument slubbered over in the compendious term, the *strange tale* of Perkin Warbeck; and the dean's whole answer comprised in two arguments, momentous no doubt, but rather more consentancous to his province of president of antiquaries, than to that of a man who attempts to reason.

The first is, that Richard murdered his nephews, *because* Edward the fifth did not walk at his uncle's coronation; and that is proved by the account, which I called the coronation-roll, not being a round but a square volume; with other such props, of which I shall take notice presently; and

The second, because sir James Tyrrel, whom, from said square book, I represented as master of the horse at Richard's coronation, was not so till some days afterwards, his younger brother occupying that place first.*

I am very thankful to our worthy president for delivering me from any alarm I might have conceived at his interposing to condemn my work. I am thankful for the arguments of mine that he chose to answer, and for those he did not choose to answer; and if it were not unbecoming the seriousness of an antiquary, and of one who in that light has the honour of being his subject, to quibble, I would say in the words of the poet,

"Blest be the gods for those they took away, And those they left me, for they left me *gay*."

Yes, I confess I did smile at so droll a delivery of the mountain; and might, I think, without impeaching, or breaking a link of the chain of my argument compliment the president with a concession of all he is so modest as to demand. Nothing prevents my offering this voluntary sacrifice, but the silly fear of having it thought that, being an antiquary, I am incapable of reasoning.

I will make a few cursory remarks on some introductory passages, and then proceed to examine Mr. President's two fulminating arguments.

The president, whose reading I confess is as it ought to be, much deeper than mine, has discovered a new author, who corroborates the murder of the two children.* This is the great Arnold, who, says the doctor, expresses in very descriptive words the manner of the young

183

princes' death. Let us hear this very expressive description. "This year decessyd the kynge (Edward 4th.) in Aprell, entring into the 23d. year of his reign, and the two sons of kynge Edward were put to silence, and the duke of Gloucester tooke upon him the crowne in July, &c." I will not observe that the duke of Gloucester is not charged with the murder, but will restrain myself to the picturesque description that so strikes the good president. I suppose he means that the children being *put to silence* implies, according to the vulgar notion, that they were smothered. May I ask whether, if their heads had been cut off, they would not equally have been *put to silence?* The Romans had a superstition of not naming death, and used various circumlocutions to avoid saying any person was dead. Did such circumlocutions imply any particular kind of death? But as the president is smitten with Arnold's painting, I will say no more in derogation of his charming eloquence, especially as it is nothing to the purpose. I doubted whether the children were murdered, not whether they were smothered or assassinated in any other way. If the doctor chooses to persist in believing they were murdered, he has my free consent to make his option of the mode. But as some of my readers may be as ignorant as I was, and not know who this pathetic historian was, we are informed in a note, that he lived in 1519, and published, not the lives or reigns of Edward the fourth, or Richard the third, but — an account of the customs of London, with a chronicle of the magistrates of that city. The thanks of the learned are due to Mr. President for thus bringing them acquainted with so valuable an author, who knew much better than

184

he who wrote the Chronicle of Croyland (an author whom doctor Milles, p. 363, allows to have been a writer of much consideration) by what kind of violent death the princes came to their end. When such an evidence as Arnold is produced to testify to a great and secret act of state, is it not evident that there is some opiniâtreté in adhering to a belief, that wants such props? As an antiquary, the dean is undoubtedly well founded in quoting our ancient classics. All my fear is, that the profane should sneer at our labours. I can admire that simplicity of antique eloquence with which we are told in a note to page 5 of the Introduction to the Archæologia, that archbishop Whitgift was *successor* to Matthew Parker, his *predecessor*; but the laughers of modern times may see no beauty in that accuracy of truth, which specifies that a man succeeded his predecessor.* Let us reserve such flowers as this, and the expressive figure of *putting to silence* for smothering, within our own penetralia for the comfort of us lovers of goodly antiquity: and perhaps it were as wise if we adhered to our own venerable lore, and to our proper province, conjectures from scraps and fragments of uninteresting matters of fact long since consigned to oblivion, instead of launching out into the bold and dangerous ocean of reasoning. I, it seems, have been shipwrecked there; and in charity, therefore, venture to warn even Mr. President himself to guide his pinnace near the coast, and only to disembark when a barrow, a tumulus, or the twinkling vestiges of a Roman camp, invite him to land and dig. Me votiva paries indicat uvida suspendisse potenti vestimenta maris Deo.

The secrecy of the murder, says the doctor, to

185

which only the few perpetrators and accomplices were privy, must have left the public under great uncertainty as to the manner, though they had no doubt as to the reality of the fact. Page 362.

Methinks this is an extraordinary position to fall from a professed advocate for the murder. Secret as it was, Arnold knew the very manner of it. The doctor must believe Arnold knew it, or he would not have quoted him for his expressive description, for the doctor cannot be absurd. But how, according to the assertors of the murder, could the public remain under great uncertainty, when those very assertors believe that Tirrel and Dighton confessed it? Do murderers confess a murder, and conceal the manner of it? May I beg to know what the doctor and his adherents do and do not believe? I protest I cannot discover. Again, in the same paragraph we are told, *that the public had no doubt as to the reality of the fact.* Strange again! Sir Thomas More and lord Bacon, the pillars that support the story, affirm over and over that there were great doubts whether one or both of the children had not escaped. Good Mr. President, ascertain your own creed, before you attempt to remove my doubts. Or is it allowable to you to reject your own authorities, and is it fair in you to insist that I should submit to them? For your own sake do not contradict yourself, only for the pleasure of contradicting me.

You proceed: "In such circumstances, absurd and even contradictory reports would arise concerning the survival and escape of these princes. Had they prevailed during the life-time of their uncle, would it not have been presumed that they were raised and propagated by him, as the best expedient for removing the suspicion of the murder?"

In such circumstances, that is, according to the preceding words, when mankind had no doubt of the reality of the fact, absurd and even contradictory reports of the survival and escape of the princes would arise. Very strange reasoning, indeed, Mr. President! Did the certainty of the murder cause men to believe that the princes were not murdered? – But let us try to fathom what the president thinks he means. In the first place, he is of opinion that the secrecy of the murder produced various reports concerning it. Then, refining on and contradicting himself, he supposes that the certainty of the murder occasioned a belief that the princes were alive; and at last he had rather that absurd and contradictory reports of their escape and survival should have been propagated by Richard himself, though he does not think such reports prevailed during Richard's life. Give me leave to ask the doctor, whether he is of all these opinions, whether he is of none, or which of them is his opinion? Let me ask him how he knows that such reports did not prevail before Richard's death? What are his authorities for dating and affixing to a subsequent period sir Thomas More's and lord Bacon's assertions, that many persons believed the children were not murdered? It is totally improbable that this should have been believed *after* Richard's death, unless there had been such an opinion *before* – for this plain reason, that it is not common to believe in the resurrections of princes. But so great is the doctor's propensity to charge Richard, that, if what he deems a falsehood had been published in Richard's time,

187

he owns he should have accused Richard as the author of it, preposterous as it would have been for Richard to have spread such tales. – Can there be stronger proof of prejudice and obstinacy?

Happy indeed would it be for the world, were tyrants and assassins no abler politicians than the good president, who thinks mankind is most easily imposed upon by absurdities and contradictions. In some cases perhaps they are; but I doubt Richard had a little more sense than to defeat his own ends by such clumsy artifices. Nor are usurpers wont to encourage a belief of the survival of their competitors, when they have thought it necessary to put those rivals to death. Henry the fourth had been disturbed by a false Richard the second; and Edward the fourth, our Richard's own brother, had chosen to expose the dead body of Henry the sixth at Paul's cross, rather than have it believed he was still living. Thus, supposing Richard had been the murderer he is represented, it is most improbable that he would have acted so sillily, as, it seems, the president would have done in his situation.

So fond is the doctor of the policy of contradictions and absurdities, that, not being able to charge them on Richard, he is determined somebody or other shall employ their machinery, and in the next sentence bestows them on the enemies of Henry the seventh, as a foundation for their pretended impostures. Here again I am sorry to be forced to ask Mr. President what he believes? Does he believe that the secrecy produced the contradictions? or that they were spread by Henry's enemies? He accounts for them one way, is willing to account for them another, and then asks with a *but*, whether it is not more probable, that they happened another way, that is not probable at all. He seems to think that in that age all men acted in a manner to defeat their own ends. According to him, Richard murders his nephews, and tells different stories of their being alive; assertions which, if false, could only operate to his prejudice, not to his service; and Henry's enemies spread as different reports of the survival of the children, which could only weaken the imposition the reporters wished to establish. Is not the murder very clear, when reduced to such shifts to preserve itself from being exploded?

In the next paragraph Mr. Buck and I are confuted, by being told that the two authors we produce to invalidate the positive account of the murder, contradict one another, *though* reporting only common hearsay. – I beg to know what Arnold did more than report common hearsay? Polidore Virgil says, it was reported that the children of Edward had escaped and were living – The continuator of the Chronicle of Croyland, that it was reported Edward's sons were dead, though it was uncertain by what kind of *violent* death. The misfortune is, that this very contradiction, so far from weakening my supposition, was the very scope of it. It was from that identical discordance among the authors who mention the fate of the children, that I attempted to show the glaring uncertainty of it. The dean perhaps thinks that the want of harmony among the evidences proves their consent. – I have known such arguments made use of on other occasions which I will not mention; but give me leave to say, that such arguments do more hurt than service to a good cause.

But Mr. Buck and I are taxed with omitting the word *violent*.* Whether Mr. Buck omitted the word violent by design or not, it is impossible for me to ascertain. For myself, I probably copied him, and was not so careful as I ought to have been in collating the passage with the original. I will, however, take any shame to myself for the omission. I had much rather confess myself in the wrong, if I am so, than be obstinate in defence of an hypothesis. Truth is too sacred to be made the victim of controversy; and I had much rather speak truth, than argue well. Indeed I must have been weaker even than I am, to have expected that I could falsify a common printed book, and not have it discovered. Could I suppose that no man living would turn to the Chronicle of Croyland? In fact, my argument does not suffer by the introduction of the word *violent*. One author says, the children were reported to be still living after the time of their supposed deaths; the other, that they were said to be dead, though it was not known by what kind of violence. What is the result, but that it was very uncertain what was become of them? If the president from two contradictory and uncertain mob-stories can strike out that certain reality of the fact, of which he affirms the public had no doubt, I own he sees further into what deduction may be drawn from an argument than I do. He proceeds yet another step; and now admitting the deposition of the Chronicle, which he had before allowed was only hearsay, as indeed the Chronicle itself confesses, by the words vulgatum est; and discovering that vulgatum est is good authority, and that in vulgus fama valuit is no authority at all, he adds, "the word *violenti* is *a*

190

most expressive and material part of the Chronicle's testimony (I do not know whether he does not perceive smothering in it), and gives a very different complexion to it." – That is, it converts vulgatum est into certain knowledge – and at last finds Richard guilty of the murder; "for if, says he, they died a violent death, there can remain no doubt by whose order it was inflicted."

Thus are we arrived at one of the grounds of the doctor's faith in the murder. My omission of the word *violenti* changes the nature of a vulgar tale into good and positive authority; and Richard, whose guilt I thought I had in some measure rendered doubtful, is convicted by my seemingly too great zeal for his character. Thus has my awkwardness dealt its blows with a two-edged sword. – I have hurt my client, and led my adversary into the intemperance of pinning his belief on what he had allowed a mob-story, for the mere satisfaction of contradicting poor me! Indeed, indeed, I am ashamed of disputing, when I am suspected of wilful omission, and see so worthy a person as the reverend divine betrayed into a perversion of reason by the idle ambition of victory in a cause of no consequence to either of us.

The learned person says, "the impartial reader of English history will judge how far the account of the murder is invalidated by the relation of Perkin Warbeck, and whether that strange tale did not gain more converts, and receive more credibility, from the natural jealousy and the affected mysterious secrecy of Henry the seventh, than from the weight of its own evidence."

As there are two propositions in this passage,

I must take leave to examine each separately. I was not the first reader of English history who was startled by the story of Perkin. Buck, Carte, Guthrie, the lord treasurer Oxford, lord Bolinbroke, and many others, had, some doubted of the murder, others been persuaded that Warbeck was the true duke of York. Even sir Thomas More and lord Bacon, the doctor's best authorities, except Arnold, had expressed the uncertainty of the murder. It was more awful testimony given by knights of the garter and privy-counsellors who had known the duke of York, who laid down their lives for that belief, and not one of whom it is even pretended by Henry's apologists recanted. Lord Bacon himself was so staggered by Henry's narrative of Perkin's confession, that he was reduced to forge a new one for him. A reader of English history must have a good digestion, and methinks not be very impartial neither, who can swallow all this without entertaining a doubt whether Perkin might not be the true duke of York. But when the readers of English history come to peruse, as I do not doubt but they will, that elaborate and ingenious treatise of Mr. Dean Milles, when they find that he believed the murder because I called a square volume a round one, and because sir James Tirrel was not master of the horse till a month after Richard's coronation, but that his brother Thomas occupied that post at the coronation; and when they find farther that so able and learned a man could not answer one argument that I had brought for Perkin being the true duke of York; will impartial readers of English history think the story perfectly clear and well ascertained? It is pretended that Perkin acknowledged himself an impostor, and that two persons confessed the murder; and yet from lord Bacon to Dr. Milles no man has been able to reconcile their accounts. The first boldly plunged into a forgery; the latter has dragged one Arnold, a writer on the customs of London, out of obscurity, to throw his mite of vulgar report into the treasury of mob-stories, and has discovered *expressive and material* authority in the vulgatum est of the Chronicle of Croyland!

The second proposition is of another nature; it is of the family of that kind of evidence which the doctor used, when he supposed Richard spread different accounts of the existence of his nephews after he had murdered them. The dean asks, whether Perkin's tale might not gain credit from the natural jealousy and affected mysterious secrecy of Henry the seventh? What can he mean by the *natural* jealousy of Henry? Was it natural to be jealous of the world's believing that his enemy was an impostor? Did he force Perkin to read a confession of being an impostor, to prevent the public from thinking him one? Because Henry's character was that of a dark mysterious tyrant, was he therefore so when it must have been destructive of his interest? Did he act in the case of Perkin as if he wanted to persuade mankind that he was not an impostor? I do not honour the abilities of Henry, but was he really so egregious a fool as the doctor paints him? For what possible reason should he endeavour to have it thought that Perkin was not an impostor? I beseech the dean, from his stores of refined policy, to tell us why Henry should have been such a blunderer? I will tell him why *he thinks* Henry was so absurd; though I cannot tell him why he ought to think so. Lord Bacon, who could not make the story of Perkin being an impostor hold together, was reduced to colour it over with the beautiful though transpicuous tints of his imposing eloquence, and accordingly tells us, *that the king's nature and customs were not greatly fit to disperse these mists, but contrariwise he had a fashion rather to create doubts, than assurance.* The charms of this vague figurative style imposed on the good president; he quotes these very words as the foundation of his opinion. The description was true with regard to Henry's conduct about his no title; but not in the least so about Perkin. The solemn phraseology however dazzled Mr. President, and he did not perceive that it contained matter contrary to fact and common sense. Read lord Bacon's own account of Henry's solicitude to detect Perkin, of the infinite pains he took to prove and publish him for an impostor, and then see if the words the doctor and I have quoted can possibly be applied to Henry's conduct on that occasion. I would wish the doctor to remember too, that when the greatest writer asserts a fact in opposition to truth and sense, he is no better authority than the lowest. If the doctor had applied his critical skill to the text he has quoted, before he bestowed it on so unworthy an object as my book, he would probably have avoided splitting on that rock. – I now come to consider his two *great* arguments.

The president opens his cause with informing his readers and me, that what I had too carelessly called the coronation-roll of Richard the third, "is not a coronation-roll, but a wardrobe-account, of which the deliveries for the coronation make a considerable part. It will be necessary, he adds, to quote several passages of this record, in order to explain the nature of it, and to judge of the evidence it contains."*

With shame I confess the truth of this charge, and with leave will relate by what means I fell into this grievous mistake, so unworthy a true antiquary. Our late learned president the bishop of Carlisle, predecessor to his present successor doctor Milles, was the first person who told me of the curious discovery made of Edward the fifth walking at his uncle's coronation, and it is with sorrow I disturb his ashes by declaring that he called this fatal wardrobe-account a coronation-roll. Another ingenious member of our society lent me an extract of the same record, and he too, I doubt, likewise called it the coronation-roll. Their cursory errors indeed do not excuse my negligence. I ought to have known that the account of the wardrobe-keeper, in which almost the whole contains deliveries for the coronation, was not the coronation-account, but the wardrobe-keeper's account for the coronation, with some other deliveries. The distinction[5] is nice, and perhaps without a difference; but as I am an antiquary, and as an antiquary is often a kind of verbal critic, hight a word-catcher, I ought to have stuck to words; the *meaning* of words is not enough. A roll implies a round volume, and lo!

5.   As in the same volume are bound accounts of the coronations of Henry the seventh and Henry the eighth, it is plain all three were reckoned in the office coronation-rolls. It was referred to doctor Milles's sagacity to discover that the office has gone on in verbal inaccuracy for above two centuries.

Words are man's province; words we teach alone.
                                        Dunciad.

195

the volume in question is square! How culpable am I in the eyes of literal accuracy! But it is time to examine the president's argument, which I take to be this.

The book is an account of the deliveries from the wardrobe from the death of Edward the fourth to some time in the following year, including the time of the intended coronation of Edward the fifth, and the actual coronation of Richard the third. As there are other deliveries previous and subsequent to the coronation of Richard, the robes ordered for Edward, under the appellation of lord Edward, son of late king Edward, were probably what had been ordered for his own coronation; and the number and similitude of the robes delivered for each king, corroborate that assertion; especially as there were half coats ordered for the henchmen of the young king, and whole coats for those of his uncle; the president having examined the account with such avidity of detecting my errors, that in the heat of the chase he stumbled on this piece of economy in Richard or his officers.

I think I have stated the whole of this first great argument with as much fairness as is possible, and it is from want of discernment if I have omitted to do justice to it. Indeed there is a very Pindaric transition from the argument to the inference; *videlicet*, that the prince was dead, if his uncle did not intend he should walk at his coronation. Was it certain Edward the fifth did walk at his uncle's coronation, it would be evident that he was not dead at the time; but would it be a proof that he was dead, if he did *not* walk there? Good Mr. Dean, this alacrity in confuting me hurries you, I fear, beyond what logic will warrant.

I will not smile at your half coats and whole coats — you concluded, to be sure, that, as Edward was a child, his henchmen must be children too, and that half the quantity would suffice them: but, to be more serious, I will as briefly as possible take to pieces your argument, after observing, that what you charge on me is far short of the express declaration of the oracle of your belief. You say that "I suppose Richard had no such evil intentions against his nephews on his accession to the crown, and that, instead of putting them to death, he meant to do honour to the eldest, by assigning him a re-spectable place, and robes of dignity at the ceremony of his coronation."

Unfortunately, instead of this being any exaggeration on my part, it is much less than your own sir Thomas More asserts to have been the intention of Richard. The chancellor tells us, on the authority of archbishop Morton, one of Richard's capital enemies, that the latter's first plan was to resign the crown to his nephew, when Edward should attain the age of 25.* Surely assigning him a place at the coronation is something less than resigning the crown to him. Had I suggested that Richard had formed any such scheme, with how much scorn should I have been treated! Sir Thomas More may give this account with impunity, and with impunity doctor Milles may choose to forget it — with impunity he may tax me with supposing less than sir Thomas More asserts — and with candour he may impute to me wilful omissions — but it shall suffice me to justify myself, and to support my arguments, with decency, and with that small portion of understanding which has fallen to my share.

The reason why I supposed it was intended Edward should walk at his uncle's coronation was simply this: Because the order for the delivery of robes to him, stands in and is mixed with the other orders for deliveries on the same occasion; and because he is there styled lord Edward, son to late king Edward the fourth.

That it is mixed with those other orders appears from the president's own account; for, having specified the other orders, and those for lord Edward, he tells us of other orders, page 373, to the duke of Buckingham, &c. for the queen's and king's coronation; and then in page 374 he says, "This paragraph seems to conclude the account of deliveries for the first coronation" – I suppose he means in opposition to the second coronation at York.*

Thus then I have established, by the dean's own testimony, that the account of deliveries to lord Edward is mixed with the other deliveries for the coronation; and by being so mixed, and being warranted by sir Thomas More to believe, that, whatever were Richard's secret intentions in futurity, he had talked of a design of delivering up the crown to his nephew on the latter's full age, was it very absurd in me to suppose, that he might carry on (to humour the doctor I will say) his hypocrisy so far as to treat his nephew with honour and respect? I wish, when we come to see the reasons assigned for Mr. Peter Curteys's inserting the deliveries to Edward amidst those for his uncle's coronation, it may not be found that wiser men have wrested the palm of absurdity from me.

But first I must produce a very material entry in this identical account, which the president has quoted without perceiving or understanding the force of it.

Antecedent to the order of deliveries to lord Edward, we find these words: "To many divers persons for to have in haste, by my lorde of Bukkingham's commandement, whose names were not remembered, delivered in grete, &c."

I ask if any man can believe that this sudden order, entered among the deliveries for the coronation of Richard, and specifying the recollection of some persons who had been omitted, was the recollection of Peter Curteys, who had forgotten to begin his account with the most obvious delivery, robes for the young king before he was set aside? or whether it was not the recollection of Richard and Buckingham, who suddenly agreed that the deposed prince should walk at his uncle's coronation? An unlucky circumstance corroborates the latter opinion. When Edward the fourth died, the duke of Buckingham was not in London, but in Wales; consequently could not direct robes for the young successor; though he was in London, and might order them against the coronation of Richard.

But what avail facts, dates, entries, arguments? The president shall wave his wand, and raise a conjecture that shall put their host to flight. In his note to page 378, this able magician owns "that many of the articles which relate to lord Edward and his hengemen are charged in the wardrobe's general account of receipts and deliveries, undistinguished from those which were issued for Richard's coronation." The confession is fair and candid, and seems almost to excuse my supposition of the nephew attending the uncle's triumph — but all shall be destroyed again. The president has a guess in store that will recover the ground he had conceded. I must beg leave to give it in his own words, for no other could do justice to it.

"The deliveries made on this account, although prior to those issued for the coronation, yet (considering the circumstances of that time) could not stand in any other place. The master of the wardrobe's account was engrossed and closed in the beginning of the following year, when the act of bastardy had passed. In what order then, or under what name or title, could these liveries be charged? They could not precede the articles for Richard's coronation, for then they must have been charged as robes for the king. Piers Courteys, no doubt, understood the *duty* of his office too well, to make so uncourtly an entry; and it would have been a dangerous experiment, at that critical period, to have excited the jealousy or resentment of his master."

"It was not for Richard's interest, nor agreeable to his inclinations, that the time or the uses for which these garments were issued, should be particularly specified. They are placed, therefore, *after the articles relative to the coronation*, amongst those issued by the king's high commandment, which in some respects was literally true. It is needless to observe, that, when this account was closed, no other title but that of lord Edward could be given to this prince."

And now I believe I may defy the wit of man, or its opposite, to produce two paragraphs, that shall pretend to argument, and be more void of common sense.*

It is plain from the two passages, that the dean felt how preposterous it would be to

200

suppose that deliveries for Edward's coronation could be crowded into the midst of that of Richard. He had owned the deliveries were so mixed as to be undistinguishable; and yet by a chicane, not quite consonant to the character of a man who accuses others of wilful omissions, and yet excusable, as it is himself he contradicts, he here asserts that they are placed *after* the articles relative to the coronation. If he forgives himself, I assure him I do. Glaring, however, as this state of the question was, any evasion, any conjecture how strained soever, was preferable to owning that deliveries for Richard's coronation *were* deliveries for Richard's coronation. How shall he avoid this dilemma? He shall begin with begging the question in dispute. He shall pronounce ex cathedrâ and of his own plenary knowledge, that *they were prior to those issued for the coronation.* Ask him how he knows this? He does not deign to tell you. But though in a pulpit or a president's chair a man may assert what he lists, without being exposed to impertinent questions, he forgot that a printed book, bestowed on the public, is liable to troublesome interrogatories, and that a man who affirms when he should argue, is likely to be proved incapable of arguing.

His next arbitrary decision is, that the deliveries for king Edward the fifth could stand in no place, but amidst the deliveries for the coronation of Richard the third. Yes, indeed, courteous reader, wonderful and extravagant as this proposition seems, if you will turn to page 379 of the Archæologia, you will find this declaration totidem verbis. How! what! you will cry – could the deliveries for Edward's coronation stand nowhere but in the account of Richard's coronation? – Is the man in his senses? Is he – But no, I hope you will not use any irreverent expressions; the dean, I assure you, is a worthy sober man, a man of good learning, I believe, and one for whom I have a very great respect; and if you will have a moment's patience, he will tell you why this matter could happen no otherwise. "The wardrobe-keeper's account was closed the next year, when king Edward had been declared a bastard by act of parliament; and therefore *in what order*, under what name or title, could the deliveries be charged? They could not precede the articles for Richard's coronation, for then they must have been charged as robes for the king," and therefore – Ay, you will cry, and therefore what? Because Edward was no longer king, did it make his intended coronation become part of Richard's coronation? Does the deposition of a king make the past acts of his reign become the acts of his successor's reign? – And you tell me this man is in his senses! Yes, indeed, kind reader, he is as much so as ever he was; and though he may not shine in argument, he is a deep antiquary, and does great honour to our society. Well, well! says the reader, all this may be so; but still, why was Richard's coronation-account the only place upon earth in which Piers Curteys could insert matters that had not only nothing to do with it, but were as opposite to it as two things could well be? Why could not the deliveries to Edward be charged *after* the articles relating to Richard? And above all, why could not Curteys charge them in their proper place, that is, previous to Richard's reign? He might have styled Edward *the lord Edward* there as well as in Richard's account: what obliged him in one page of the same book to call a man king, whom in another page of the very same book he calls lord? A child of ten years old would reason better. Gentle reader, all this is very true; and yet we are not arrived at the most entertaining part of the argument. The dean, who has all along argued as if Richard the third and Henry the seventh had been two drivellers, has not more mercy on poor Peter Curteys, though meaning him very well, and lending him all his own share of policy. Piers Curteys, says he, no doubt understood the *duty* of his office too well to make so *uncourtly* an entry; that is, *before* Richard's coronation. Whatever Curteys understood, it is plain the dean thinks he did not understand keeping his accounts, when he blended and confounded matters foreign to one another in such a manner, that to this day the dean cannot unravel them. I am indeed more surprised to hear a reverend divine call it *the duty of office* to make a false entry: and this arch dislocation of the wardrobe-keeper's accounts, the dean ascribes to Curteys's *adroitness in paying his court*. Clergymen, I say it to their honour, have ever been observed to be woful courtiers, and to have often blundered into affronting princes, from their over officiousness in flattering them. What an expedient has the dean lighted on to prevent Curteys from offending Richard, by reminding him that he had dispossessed the king his nephew! Thus must the courtly Curteys have argued, according to the dean's notions of kings and courtiers, and cunning: If I charge my deliveries to Edward, says Curteys to himself, in their due time and place, it will imply that Edward has been king, and that his uncle has dethroned him. Richard is a jealous, suspicious, shrewd and cruel prince, and may put me to death for my veracity. Well! but is there no private place, no obscure corner, not likely to be noticed, into which I can slide my account for Edward, and which will escape the piercing eye of Richard? Oh! yes, there is one, and indeed the only one where it can stand properly, from the excess of the impropriety, and where from that very impropriety it will never be observed. I will place Edward's account in the midst of Richard's coronation-account, and then the devil is in it if he will discover it — nay, and to conceal my artifice still better, I will call Edward, not king, but the lord Edward, son of the late king — a title so descriptive of his situation, and dispossession by Richard, that it will be impossible Richard should ever recollect he dispossessed him.

Thus has the dean removed all difficulties, *thus* has he confuted my *strange* supposition, that an article in the midst of an account for a particular service relates to that particular service, and to that service only. Were I fond of disputation, could I desire better fortune than to have always such adversaries? Abilities must be poor indeed, to which opponents of that force would not prove a foil, and give seeming brightness. Yet I venture to foretell that there will not be wanting men whose heads are so adapted to false reasoning, that the doctor's arguments will instantly strike them with the most luminous conviction: for absurdities, when they light on a proper soil, resemble some of the seeds in the parable, *which falling upon stony places, forthwith sprung up, because they had no deepness of earth.* But I shall say no more on this head, and shall be far more brief on the second great article of the dean's observations. As his mode of argumentation was arrived at its perfection in the famous passages above quoted, he could not soar any higher; and indeed the second article, in comparison of the first, is very flat, and tastes more of the antiquary than the logician.

I have said, that in the account of Richard's coronation it appeared that sir James Tirrel walked as master of the horse, and thence inferred that he was a considerable officer of the crown at that time, and consequently of too great rank to be named as an obscure person, and recommended by a still more obscure person, a nameless page, as a proper instrument for a secret murder: and I showed that sir Thomas More, who tells this absurd story on nameless authority, had added another falsity, which was in saying that Tirrel was not knighted till after the supposed assassination.

The dean is so impartial as to give up sir Thomas's falsification or blunder in regard to the knighthood – so in one respect at least I am allowed to have discovered that sir Thomas spoke with little knowledge of the person he described – but the dean, who has studied and pondered over, and tortured the wardrobe-account to make it depose against me, has discovered, that it was not sir James Tirrel who walked at Richard's coronation as master of the horse, but his younger brother sir Thomas; and that the latter was not master of the horse, but only occupied the office of master of the horse at that time; though both the president and the book are forced to confess that sir James was actually master of the horse before the second coronation at York, which happened but two months afterwards.*

This important point gained, the president concludes, that what he calls this promotion coinciding exactly in point of time with sir Thomas More's account of the murder, it is most probable that the mastership of the horse was bestowed on sir James Tirrel, as a reward for the black service that he had just committed; and that his own brother was set aside, or, in his words, superseded, to make way for him.

Not satisfied, however, with this wonderful discovery, the president modestly bestows collateral helps, as buttresses to his argument. The first is an assertion by implication. The delivery of the stable furniture to him, says he, *implies* his having then *first* taken possession of his office. Methinks this painful accuracy implies a little suspicion that sir James Tirrel had been named master of the horse a little earlier. Is not a man master of the horse from the moment of the king's nomination, though he may not have taken possession of the stables and saddles? If the dean will send to the office, he will soon see how futile this *verbal* precision is.

The second buttress is more in character, though, if possible, still less to the purpose. It is an ample pedigree of the Tirrels for five descents, and is set forth and guarantied by all the pomps of impertinent heraldry – and only to prove what no mortal disputes, and what ascertains no part of the argument, namely, that sir James and sir Thomas Tirrel were brothers.*

But though I veil my bonnet with all due deference to the president's genealogic abilities, he will excuse me, if I have not quite the same deference for his arguments, which, with submission, I shall now show to be as ill-grounded as his conjectures.

The very expression that the younger brother *occupied* the office of master of the horse, and that the elder *was* master of the horse in less than two months, would have struck any other man but the president, I believe, that the younger brother officiated for the elder. But this is nothing to the inference the president draws from this imaginary disgrace of the junior. It immediately makes him see, that while the younger was executing this high employment, the elder was an obscure fellow, of little note, and therefore proper to be recommended by one does not know whom, as a ready villain, proper for an assassination. He was, indeed, "master of the king's hengemen or pages; consequently it was his duty to be attendant on the king, and probably to sleep in his antichamber, whilst the pages themselves were employed in menial offices nearer the royal person." These are the dean's words; and he adds, it is in no respect improbable that he should be seen in the king's antichamber, where Richard first proposed to him the murder of his two nephews.

Now must I ask the dean seriously, whether it was from not understanding his own language, or from wilful perversion of my words, that he pretends I argued as if I thought it not likely that sir James Tirrel might be seen in Richard's antichamber. I never said any such thing: whoever will read my book will see I never used so silly an argument; and I must repeat, the dean wilfully or ignorantly mistakes my words when he ascribes such a meaning to them.

I said, and I repeat it, that sir James Tirrel

was an officer of too high rank to be described in the absurd manner by which he is painted by sir Thomas More. I said, and I repeat it, that there is not common sense in the tale there told; that an usurper would not go to Warwick to dispatch orders for a murder to be committed in London, which he had just left, without taking any steps towards the murder. I said, that it was not likely that a page should recommend a great officer of the crown to the king for an assassin; and it was still less likely, as sir James was already in great favour with his master. I ask the dean, who is so able a courtier and politician, whether he thinks a menial servant would recommend for a murder one of the principal officers of the court? And I am so hardy as still to call sir James Tirrel so, though he did not *occupy* the office of master of the horse till two months after the time I had assigned. Master of the hengemen was a place of great trust – that master of the hengemen was brother to the person who at least then officiated as master of the horse: and what is worse, Mr. President, who unfortunately does not perceive the importance of the materials he handles, owns that sir James, in the reign of Edward the fourth, had been a commissioner for executing – what? – the office of high-constable of England, the first office in the kingdom, an office suppressed by Henry the eighth on account of its dangerous and almost unbounded power; and he owns likewise that sir James had been made a knight banneret by Richard in Scotland that very year – and be it noticed, that bannerets were created only by the king or commander in chief, when they themselves were present in the field; and that nothing but signal bravery entitled any man in those martial ages to so distinguished an honour. After this, the dean or any man else is welcome to believe, that when Richard bemoaned himself to one of his pages that he could not find an assassin, the said nameless page replied, "Sir, there lieth one in the palet-chamber without that I dare say will do your grace pleasure; the thing were right hard that he would refuse."

But I have not done with Mr. President yet; I must task him a little farther. Though he owned that I detected sir Thomas More in one falsification, how comes he himself to quote him for another, in which I had detected him likewise? Sir Thomas More had said that Tirrel "had a high heart, and sore longed upwards, not rising so fast as he hoped, being hindered and kept under by sir Richard Ratcliffe and sir William Catesby." I had showed the impossibility of this being true, and also that Ratcliffe was absent at Pontefract. Where is the dean's candour in suppressing that detection? Does he think he avoids it by quoting Hall, instead of sir Thomas More, though Hall uses More's own words?

But before the president can wind up my complete confutation, he is so kind as to furnish me with another instance of his judgment, which I cannot pass by. In pinning down sir James Tirrel's promotion to the precise moment established by More, he drops these words: It happened "immediately before the creation of Richard's son, prince of Wales, an event to which the lives of the two princes seemed to be the only obstacle."* Mr. President, your readers and I must again ask whether you know what you say? Do you commonly argue in this manner? What! were they an obstacle to the father's making his son prince of Wales, when they had not been an obstacle to his making himself king? For what reason? How, why were they an obstacle? Deign to inform us – or, if you cannot, as I firmly believe you cannot, I will inform you how they might be an obstacle, though you will not like the reason – and yet you ought to like it, for it is again drawn from your oracle sir Thomas More. If Richard, as sir Thomas asserts, had insinuated that he intended to restore the crown to his eldest nephew, it would have been a most hasty and indecent contradiction to have created his son prince of Wales. Thus you see how you ought to have argued; and you may see too, that when you get hold of a good argument, it is without knowing it. In the mean time you have reduced yourself to this alternative: if Richard did not pretend, or had not pretended to intend to restore his nephew, there is no sense in saying that there was more reason for not making his own son prince of Wales, than there had been for making himself king. If he did pretend such a design, then treating his nephew with honour, and exhibiting him at his own coronation as king in futuro, was but part of the same policy, and is confirmed by the entry of deliveries for Edward in the account of Richard's coronation. You have allowed that Richard deferred creating his son prince of Wales, as is certain; but you avoid the only obvious reason for it, and have recourse to one that is no reason at all.

I will go a step farther, sir, and assist you a little in your confutation – nay, if you provoke me, I will answer my book myself, to show you how you should have answered it. Do not you then perceive, sir, that my hypothesis of Edward's walking at his uncle's coronation by no means destroys the supposed murder? You have been so rash as to pin it down to the precise moment assigned by sir Thomas More, which is incredible: but had you admitted, according to the wardrobe-account, that Edward walked, or it was intended should walk, at his uncle's investiture, you would have exhibited Richard as an artful usurper, instead of making him the clumsy fool he appears in your and sir Thomas's narrative. When he treated his nephew with honour, produced him in robes like his own, talked of restoring the crown to him, and refrained from declaring his own son his successor, he acted like an artful politican, and might hope to blind the people by this hypocrisy, and give a better colour to his nephew's death, if he intended afterwards to take him off, and give out that he died a natural death. Which was the case I have never pretended to say. That he murdered the younger brother, is another question; and I fear, sir, you must confute all I have said on Perkin Warbeck, before you will be able to establish the affirmative. At present you will excuse me if I do not assist you in that task too, till I find you a more hopeful scholar.

And now to conclude – Do you really expect that your readers will believe the murder, because I called a square book a roll, because Piers Curteys charged his deliveries in the most improper place in which he could place them, and because you have produced a pedigree of the Tirrels? I say nothing of your arguments, because I think you will adhere to any thing rather than to them. Or shall I be persuaded that it was not intended Edward the fifth should walk at Richard's coronation, though you have corroborated all my reasons for believing so?* And shall I give up a long chain of argument, founded on the absurdities, falsehoods and contradictions of your authorities, and supported by facts and dates? No, sir, I am sure you are too modest to make such a request; and though out of deference to you I have done what I had declared I would not do, that is, answer two or three immaterial and detached cavils, picked and culled out of at least a dozen pages of arguments, as I have drawn them up at the end of my work; and though you have used all your endeavours in sifting and torturing the coronation-roll (for I again dare to call it so), to make it refute me, yet I cannot pay you the compliment of saying that you have satisfied one of my doubts. If the book deserved the honour of being answered by you, it deserved to be answered like a man. Take it, show the weakness of it, pull the arguments to pieces from beginning to end: make sense of the tale of Perkin — it is a stale shift in controversy to bestow names instead of arguments, especially when we cannot answer. Prove that Perkin was an impostor; it is below you to avoid the challenge by calling it a strange tale. For your own sake, and for the honour of the society, I wish to see a better answer to my work stand in our Memoirs than that you have tacked to the first volume. I shall rejoice at it, though you have acted so differently from what you yourself have pronounced a merit in your predecessor; in whose panegyric, page lxiii, you say, "His literary merit with the society received an additional lustre from the affability of his temper, the gentleness of his manners, and the benevolence of his heart, *which united every* *member of the society in esteem to their head,* and in harmony and friendship to each other." The late bishop of Carlisle, I am apt to think, would not have deemed controversy the nursing mother of concord. Indeed, sir, had I seen your Observations previously to their publication, I should have been strangely divided in my inclinations – for my own sake, I should have wished you to publish them; for yours, to suppress them. You have saved me from a difficulty, and I thank you; and, as a proof of my gratitude, I wish to see a mitre adorn your brow. The most exemplary fathers of the church have not always been the best logicians.

Aug. 28, 1770

FINIS

SHORT OBSERVATIONS ON THE REMARKS OF THE REV. MR. MASTERS ON THE HISTORIC DOUBTS
Published in the second Volume of the Archæologia

A new knight having entered the lists in the controversy concerning Richard III. I shall bestow a few words on his notes, though with much circumspection; for, although he professes to condemn me, he has contributed so much to the discomfit of my adversaries, that I cannot but be obliged to him for having furnished me with new weapons, which though he brought into the field against me, he has, by mistake, directed against them. Why he opposes me, though thinking as I do, I cannot tell; perhaps he can. It shall be my business notwithstanding to set him right, and to show him that his arguments, as far as they have any meaning, support mine, and tend to confirm my doubts.

He says I assert facts on the slightest evidence against the common current of almost all the cotemporary historians.

Answer. There were but two cotemporary historians, Fabian, and the author of the Chronicle of Croyland. I have quoted the first to show that Richard did not murder Edward prince of Wales, son of Henry VI. and to the second I have appealed for the same cause and many other facts. I have laid the same stress on the continuator of the Chronicle as Mr. Masters

214

does (vide p. 16 of Hist. Doubts). Is this the proof of my rejecting his authority?

Fabian says prince Edward was slain by the king's servants – Mr. Masters concludes *servants* mean *great men*; but they must mean the king's brothers too, or Richard, even from Fabian's words, cannot be included in the charge. Mr. Masters, to prove *servants* mean what the term cannot mean, *the king's own brothers*, produces the phrase I had quoted from the Chronicle, *ultricibus quorundam manibus*; and in that very phrase too finds the *quorundam* to mean *the king's brothers*: that is, he finds that the lowest term implies the highest. Was I in the wrong to say that he is on my side without knowing it? Or will he be so good as to quote a passage in any tolerable author, in which such a term as *somebody or other* is used to signify the first men in a nation? If an historian, describing the death of Hotspur at the battle of Shrewsbury, had said, *he was slain by one knows not whom*, should we have ever guessed that he was killed by Henry prince of Wales?

As in the next article, the murder of Henry VI, Mr. Masters seems not to know his own opinion, I shall pass it over without a remark.*

On the murder of Clarence he is equally uncertain. But he thinks my argument drawn from Edward's complaint of no man's interceding for Clarence, confutes the authorities I have quoted for Richard's openly resisting Clarence's death. If intercession and open resistance are synonimous terms, I own I have argued ill: if they are not, Mr. Masters does not argue very well.

But I have called in question the authority of sir Thomas More's History. True, I have; and

215

Rastell's Chronicle, written many years after by sir Thomas More's own brother-in-law, shows that I had some reason for so doing. If sir Thomas's account received from archbishop Morton was authentic, could it be doubtful so many years afterwards? Is it credible that Rastell should never have seen sir Thomas's History? And if it was genuine, could Rastell, brother and printer to its author, give two other different accounts of the deaths of Edward V. and his brother? Were More and Rastell so nearly allied and so intimate, and yet did neither communicate his work to the other? When Rastell wrote his Chronicle, would not sir Thomas have asked, why he reported vague, absurd and improbable tales of their deaths, when he himself had given the only certain account from the best authority? When Rastell did not believe the narrative of his own brother-in-law, am I so very culpable for questioning it? If Mr. Masters was good at reconciling contradictions, I would entreat him to solve these. Till he had, I must beg leave to rank him on my side; as he must either doubt with me, or believe contradictions.

I am again warranted to claim this gentleman as the supporter of my opinion, by his owning on p. 204 that the parliament-roll (which I have quoted, but, with leave, never plumed myself on having discovered) asserts the pre-contract of Edward IV. with the lady Eleanor Butler. But Mr. Masters goes much farther; and, to the confusion of our antagonists, shows that she probably broke her heart on the king's marriage. I should not have been bold enough to go so far, but am obliged to him for taking that task on himself. Why he says a few lines higher, that it might as well have been Lucy as Butler,

216

when he has proved it was Butler, I cannot conceive. But as he assists me with new proofs, I will not quarrel with him for a disposition to contradict me.

I am sorry his arguments against me are weaker than the facts he furnishes me with – but what can I say to such reasoning as this? If *lady Eleanor Butler was dead, as she certainly was, long before the birth of Edward V. this surely could not be a proper foundation of his illegitimacy*, p. 205. I will not dwell on the context of this argument, which is, that if she was not dead when Edward V. was born, it would have been a foundation for bastardizing him; which implies that she had been married to Edward IV. – But can a divine really know so little of the canon law, as to think that the death of a lawful wife legitimates ipso facto the issue of children born of an illegal wife? If lady Eleanor Butler was Edward's lawful wife, lady Gray could not become his lawful wife by a marriage performed during lady Eleanor's life. To make her his lawful wife, he must have married her again on Eleanor's death, or the pope must at least have legitimated her children. Even in these times an illegal marriage does not become a valid one, unless, as lady Wishfor't says, by an iteration of nuptials. A very recent and celebrated cause confirms this doctrine. Did not the last earl of Anglesea marry his second wife again after the death of the first?

What the scope or even the meaning of the next paragraph is, I protest I cannot comprehend. What is the meaning of lady Catherine Stafford marrying her father's grandson?* In English, it would imply that she married her nephew. Did she? In Edmondson's Peerage, I find that lady Catherine Stafford had by John

217

Talbot earl of Shrewsbury a daughter named Anne, wife of the lord Boteler or Butler of Sudley. As there appears no other female Talbot who married a lord Butler, it was natural to suppose that the christian name of *Anne* was put for Catherine; a mistake so common in voluminous genealogies, that no man of sense can wonder at it. Dugdale says the same, and makes the lady Butler grand-daughter of the duke of Buckingham – Thus, if Buck misled me, Dugdale misled him. But Raphe Brooke, p. 196, makes Eleanor lady Butler, as Mr. Masters does, daughter of John Talbot first earl of Shrewsbury by his second wife Margaret Beauchamp. Indeed Brooke, nor any man else, I believe, but Mr. Masters ever said that a woman was *descended* from her own father. Mr. Masters, taking half of my argument for the whole, by a licence frequent in controversy, says, that to magnify her descent I make her of the royal family: I have said *she was sister of the earl of Shrewsbury, one of the greatest peers in the kingdom, and grand-daughter of the duke of Buckingham, a prince of the blood; an alliance in that age never reckoned unsuitable.* I could not be absurd enough to say a princess of the blood was in that age not reckoned a match unsuitable to the crown. I must have meant that a sister of one great peer and grand-daughter of another descended from Edward III. must have struck the nation as a properer match for the king than the widow Gray – and Mr. Masters, with his usual kindness in assisting me, affirms that lady Eleanor was grand-daughter of the great Beauchamp earl of Warwick, and niece of the duchess of Norfolk, besides being daughter of the first hero of the age. Are not my arguments wonderfully invalidated by such contradiction?

For the wardrobe-account, I will refer the reader to my answer to Dr. Milles. For the rest of Mr. Masters's opinions, containing neither new facts nor arguments, I shall leave them to make for or against me as they may. One instance of his candour I will mention. I have asked why the evidence of the queen-mother, of her daughters, and of a thousand others who had seen Richard duke of York in his childhood, was not demanded to prove that Perkin Warbeck was an impostor. Mr. Masters has discovered that the queen-dowager was dead: and one of a legion being dead, he thinks it very fair to set aside all the rest. It is just what has been done by all my answers. They have picked and culled disjointed passages here and there, jumped at a trifling anachronism or two, shunned, carefully shunned the thread of the argument, dreaded and fled from the repeated question on Tirrel's evidence, on which I offered to rest the whole, and taken care to make no reply to the table of arguments that I have recapitulated at the end. Instead of this manly mode of logical argumentation, they have recourse to clamours on great names, and ask me how I dare dispute the authorities of such men as More and Bacon? Mr. Masters, the last of my answerers, is even offended that I laugh at three chancellors. I hope a fourth will reward Him, and then I shall laugh at four.

But I have not incurred this gentleman's displeasure for making free with chancellors alone: he feels even for popish bishops, and in p. 214 reproves my reflections on the catholic clergy who condemned Jane Shore. Yet the very censures that I pass on *holy persons*, are decent, commendable, in sound divines. A holy person

219

may call downright names; with impunity he may, in very coarse terms, abuse a prelate, who was both bishop and *chancellor*. In short, Mr. Masters, in p. 206, says of doctor Stillington bishop of Bath and chancellor, that he was a time-serving, revengeful prelate, and acted the part of a pimp to king Edward. That I despise *monkish* historians is most certain, (v. p. 200 of the Archæol.) and for these reasons, because they are partial, bigoted to authority, inaccurate, and generally incapable of reasoning: because they illiberally vilify those who are not of their opinion, and yet deny the smallest liberty of censure to others: and, above all, because they prefer absurd traditions to the investigation of truth, and cannot see a sun beam break into their cell, without being ready to cry Fire! So much do they apprehend the detection of error, so much do they think faith and darkness involved in one common cause. Sir Thomas More and lord Bacon repeat over and over that the murders of the children were uncertain. The true believers, that is the credulous, insist on believing that More and Bacon believed what they say they did not believe, for could they believe what they declare was uncertain? Was it possible for two men of such acute and penetrating genius as More and Bacon to believe that a king and his brother were murdered, that the crime was confessed by the perpetrators, and yet that the fact remained uncertain? A monkish historian may relate such a legend, but one must be a monk or an antiquary to give him credit.

Here therefore I take my leave of All who think credulity in ancient fables a cousin-german of faith, and that great names can legitimate bastard tales by having stood god-fathers to them, even though the sponsors have registered their doubts on the spuriousness of the babes they have ushered into the world.

Whilst I had the honour of being member of the Society of Antiquaries, I used my weak endeavours to promote the study of antiquities by publishing ancient pieces really valuable or intrinsically curious; at the same time taking the liberty of blending criticism and free discussion with the passion I had for the remains of past ages; not having quite so much superstition or bigotry as to think that time can stamp value on every thing it has spared, merely by not having destroyed it. I went so far as to hold, that popular lies do not acquire the force of truth solely by having been handed down to us – an opinion, which I confess does not a little clash with the dignity of oral tradition. I have found my error: the president of our learned society, and the reverend Mr. Masters, disapproved of my making common sense the touchstone of legends which two great men had adopted, and three centuries had consecrated. The immortal volumes of our society, the *Archæologia*, which I was once so irreverent as to interpret *old women's logic*, will for ever record my condemnation. The tales, which the acute sceptic Hume thought himself called upon in honour to uphold, only because he had from idleness adopted them, are now irrefragably established in the annals of the society, amidst so many profound researches and conjectures on Danish inscriptions, and Saxon epitaphs in Latin on obscure Romish priests, those relics of ignorant and barbarous ages, of late become the darling occupation of the learned. Richard the

Third and I are left to the mercy of that futile posterity, who shall be content with the trifling amusement of reasoning and argumentation; while the more enlightened shall be sustained in their faith by the authority of such great names as those of More, Bacon, Milles, and Masters.

Convinced of my unworthiness to fill a seat in so solid an assembly, I resigned my place: and though I shall no more disturb the repose of their *crudite* and *recondite* volumes, I shall wait with impatience for the moment when the venerable academy shall oblige the public with their lucubrations on the history of Whittington and his cat.[6]

6. Though the author pays the society the compliment of having left them on a sense of his own unworthiness, he did not really withdraw his name from their register, till their consultation on the story of Whittington and his cat had been brought on the stage by Foote, and had made them ridiculous; as the author of these pages intimated in a letter to their secretary; not thinking he was obliged to share in the ridicule of follies, in which he had no part. H.W.

POSTSCRIPT TO MY HISTORIC DOUBTS
Written in February 1793

It is afflictive to have lived to find in an age called not only civilized but enlightened, in this eighteenth century, that such horrors, such unparalleled crimes have been displayed on the most conspicuous theatre in Europe, in Paris the rival of Athens and Rome, that I am forced to allow that a multiplicity of crimes, which I had weakly supposed were too manifold and too absurd to have been perpetrated even in a very dark age, and in a northern island not only not commencing to be polished, but enured to barbarous manners, and hardened by long and barbarous civil wars amongst princes and nobility strictly related – Yes, I must *now* believe that any atrocity may have been attempted or practised by an ambitious prince of the blood aiming at the crown in the fifteenth century. I *can* believe (I do not say I do) that Richard duke of Gloucester dipped his hand in the blood of the saint-like Henry the sixth, though so revolting and injudicious an act as to excite the indignation of mankind against him. I can now believe that he contrived the death of his own brother Clarence – and I can think it possible, inconceivable as it was, that he aspersed the chastity of his own mother, in order to bastardize the offspring of his eldest brother; for all these extravagant excesses have been exhibited in the compass of five years by a monster, by a royal duke, who has actually surpassed all the guilt imputed to Richard the third, and who, devoid of Richard's courage, has acted his enormities openly, and will leave it impossible to any future writer, however disposed to candour, to entertain one *historic doubt* on the abominable actions of Philip duke of Orleans.

After long plotting the death of his sovereign, a victim as holy as, and infinitely superior in sense and many virtues to, Henry VI. Orleans has dragged that sovereign to the block, and purchased his execution in public, as in public he voted for it.

If to the assassination of a brother (like the supposed complicity of Gloucester to that of Clarence) Orleans has not yet concurred; still, when early in the revolution he was plotting the murder of the king, being warned by an associate that he would be detected, he said, "No; for I will have my (natural) brother the abbé de St. Far stabbed too, and then nobody will suspect me of being concerned in the murder of my own brother." – So ably can the assassins of an enlightened age refine on and surpass the atrocious deeds of Goths and Barbarians!

Shade of Richard of Gloucester! if my weak pen has been able to wash one bloody speck, one incredible charge from *your* character, can I but acknowledge that Philip of Orleans has sullied my varnish, and at least has weakened all the arguments that I drew from the improbability of *your* having waded so deeply into wickedness and impudence that recoiled on yourself, as to caluminate your own mother with adultery. If *you* did, it was to injure the children of your brother – still *you* had not the senseless, shameless effrontery to shake your own legitimacy. – Philip of Orleans mocks your pitiful self-partiality – He in person, and not by proxy, has declared his own mother a strumpet, has bastardized himself, and for ever degraded his children as progeny descended from a coachman! – For what glory, for what object, far be it from me to conjecture! – Who would have a mind congenial enough to that of such a monster, as to be able to guess at his motives?

FINIS

NOTES TO THE TEXT

A number of notes have been added to the text to explain or correct some of Walpole's statements. Since this is not a full new edition no attempt has been made to correct his interpretations nor to identify or verify all quotations from his various sources. A short bibliography of books used by Walpole is added at the end, (although sometimes in modern editions and not necessarily in the editions which he used), so that references can be checked if desired. The books referred to in the notes to the introduction and to the text have also been included.

P. 14.   Walpole's omission here of the *History of England* by William Guthrie aroused one of his severer critics, see p. xi.

P. 15.   See 'Supplement', below p. 223.

P. 16.   This 'crime' is certainly not now laid at Richard's door. See Charles Ross, *Richard III* (1981), p. 22.

P. 18.   It is now generally accepted that if Richard of Gloucester was in the Tower on the night Henry VI died, it was as a messenger for his brother Edward, see Ross op. cit. p. 22.

P. 20.   There is no doubt that Anne was married to Edward of Lancaster, see P.M. Kendall, *Richard the Third*), p. 106.

P. 21.   That Gloucester resisted the execution of Clarence is corroborated by Dominic Mancini, writing in 1483, (*The Usurpation of Richard III*, 1969, p. 63). For the butt of Malmsey see pp. 63, 111.

P. 22.   This topic has been discussed extensively since Walpole's day, see for example Ross, op. cit., Kendall, op. cit., and the excellent summary in the *Complete Peerage*, vol. 12, Part 2, Appendix J.

P. 23.   In fact aged 10.

P. 23.   There are others, see for example Mancini (note 6 above), which has come to light since Walpole wrote, and those discussed in Alison Hanham, *Richard III and his early historians* (1975).

P. 23.   It is now generally accepted that the author of the *Chronicle*, whoever he was, probably did have inside information on events. See the chapter on authorship of the Chronicle in Nicholas Pronay and John Cox, *The Crowland Chronicle Continuations, 1463–1487* (1986), pp. 78–99 passim.

P. 24   This theory is supported by the most recent editor of More, see R.S. Sylvester, *The History of King Richard III* (Yale 1963), pp. lxxx–civ.

P. 30.   For a chronology of events from 9 April to 26 June 1483 see Anne F. Sutton and P.W. Hammond, *The Coronation of Richard III* (1983), pp. 13–25.

P. 33   So far as is known Hastings stayed in London throughout the crisis.

P. 36.   Probably not openly.

P. 42.   Actually BL Harleian Manuscript 433 f.2b. Article 6 is the number given this item in the 1759 Catalogue.

P. 45.   It seems probable that Eleanor Butler was the sister of the Earl of Shrewsbury, but that her mother was Ankaret Strange, daughter of John Lord Strange of Blackmere, not Katherine Stafford. See note to p. 217.

P. 46.   Robert Masters accused Walpole of claiming the discovery of the Rolls of Parliament. He was obviously doing nothing of the kind.

P. 50.   On 13 June, see Chronology referred to above, (see note to p. 30), pp. 21, 23.

P. 51.   Haute was not executed with Rivers, Vaughan and Grey, see Anne F.Sutton, 'The Hautes of Kent', *The Ricardian*, 1982, vol. 6, p. 55.

P. 52.   Richard dated his reign from 26 June 1483.

P. 55.   In fact on 17 July.

P. 56.   Not a second Coronation but the installation of his son Edward as Prince of Wales.

P. 57.   It seems probable that Sir James Tyrell was in fact Master of the Horse at Richard's Coronation, although the Great Wardrobe account says Thomas Tyrell. This was pointed out by Milles, see p. 183 below.

P. 59.   Tyrell was executed for treason in 1502. Walpole made attempts to locate Tyrell's attainder, having the Rolls of Parliament searched for the purpose (letter from Joseph Edmondson, 26 July 1767, Yale, vol. 41, p. 92).

P. 60.   See note to p. 56 above.

P. 65.   Richard created his son Prince of Wales on 24 August 1483.

P. 66.   The Great Wardrobe account for the period. It includes all the robes and other necessities ordered for the Coronation, and some ordered for the Coronation of Edward V, hence the entry Walpole refers to. For an edition of this document see Sutton and Hammond, *The Coronation of Richard III*, pp. 47–190.

P. 67.   She was in the Great Wardrobe before going into Sanctuary.

P. 69.   There is only one 'Croyland' author, the 'continuator'.

P. 70.   More accessibly see P.W. Hammond and Anne F. Sutton, *Richard III: the Road to Bosworth Field* (1983), pp. 154–9. The words quoted by Walpole appear in the part of the Act presented to Richard of Gloucester in June 1483, when the Princes were certainly alive. Walpole owned a transcript copy of this Act, (see Yale, vol. 41, pp. 92–93).

P. 73.   This letter (see George Buck, *The History of King Richard the Third* (1979), p. 191), has never been seen subsequently.

P. 80.   In fact in 1473.

P. 85.   Lady Catherine Gordon, see p. 124 below.

P. 85.   For the most detailed account of Perkin Warbeck see James Gairdner, *History of the Life and Reign of Richard the Third* (1898), pp. 263–335.

P. 89.   It is not generally accepted that Perkin Warbeck was the Duke of York, but it has never been proved that he was not.

P. 95.   The date of composition usually accepted now is 1514–1518, i.e. in the reign of Henry VIII.

P. 98.   For a discussion of the Countess of Desmond see P.W. Hammond, 'The Appearance of Richard III', in *Richard III: Crown and People*, edited by J.O. Petre, (1985), pp. 3–4.

P. 99.   Copied by Vertue from the original in the Salisbury Roll. See photograph in John Harvey, *The Plantagenets* (1948), figure 74.

P. 100.   Richard was born on 2 October 1452, and was thus nearly 33 when he died.

P. 100.   Quoted in full in Gairdner, *History of the Life and Reign of Richard the Third* (1898), p. 5.

P. 103.   This was an error, see below, p. 136.

P. 106.   This is an error by Drake, (and Buck), for John of Gloucester, the only proven illegitimate son of Richard III.

P. 107.   This is John of Gloucester.

P. 107.   For a discussion of the illegitimate children Richard III see P.W. Hammond, 'The Illegitimate Children of Richard III', in *Richard III: Crown and People*, ed. J.O. Petre, (1985), pp. 18–23.

P. 108.   This interpretation of the play is not usually accepted.

P. 111.   Actually BL Harleian Ms.433 f.340b, article 2378 in the 1758 Catalogue of the Harleian manuscripts.

P. 112.   'Jane' Shore was probably divorced, at her own suit, from William Shore in 1476. She certainly married Thomas Lynom *c.* 1483, see Nicholas Barker, 'Jane Shore', in *Etoniana* (no. 125, 1972), pp. 388, 389.

P. 130.   See Introduction, p. ii.

P. 135.   No such record exists.

P. 136.   See above, p. 103.

P. 136.   This was 'FWG', see above, p. xi.

P. 136.   The critic 'Impartialis', see above, p. x.

P. 139.   The review was by Edward Gibbon, see above, p. xii.

P. 140.   For Walpole's feelings towards these notes by Hume, see above, p. xii.

P. 142.   Walpole translates from Gibbon's review. The text differs slightly from that afterwards published in Hume's *History of England* (1789), vol. 3, note M.

P. 146.   For Tyrell's position as Master of the Horse see note to p. 57 above.

P. 157.   Hume's list, as well as the Queen includes the Marquis Dorset, Sir Thomas St Leger, Sir Giles Daubeney, the Cheneys and the Stanleys, all of whom certainly afterwards supported Henry Tudor.

P. 160.   Hume's note (from the English version), says 'He [Richard] knew, therefore her title to be good: for as to the declaration of her illegitimacy, as it went upon no proof, or even pretence of proof, it was always regarded with the utmost contempt by the nation . . .'

P. 161.   Hume is arguing here that Richard's silence concerning the whereabouts of his nephews makes it likely that he could not say anything, and must therefore have murdered them.

P. 166.   Hume argues that Warbeck's 'imposture' was organised by the Duchess of Burgundy. His actual words about Carte are 'It is remarkable that Mr Carte, in order to preserve the weight of testimony in favour of Perkin, suppresses entirely this material fact [Margaret's support for Simnel]; a strong effect of party predjudice and this author's desire of blackening Henry VII, whose hereditary title to the crown was defective.'

P. 170.   These bones are those discovered in the Tower in the reign of Charles II, of two young people of approximately the correct ages to be the sons of Edward IV. They were only examined scientifically in 1933, and then not properly. A full examination is long overdue, see P.W. Hammond and W.J. White, 'The Sons of Edward IV' in *Richard III: Loyalty, Lordship and Law*, edited by P.W. Hammond, (1986), pp. 104–147.

P. 172.   This may possibly be the anonymous correspondent who wrote a very long letter to Walpole in December 1767, having seen the announcements for *Historic Doubts* (Yale, vol. 41, pp. 111–115). The letter made very similar points to those Walpole made in his book.

P. 173.   Now known as the Rous Roll, and in the British Library, (Additional MS. 48976), see John Rous, *The Rous Roll* (1980). The engravings Walpole refers to were published in

229

the *Complete Works* (1798), vol. 2, p. 166.

P. 174.   Cap. 63 of the edition cited above.

P. 174.   Walpole's version was the 'English' roll. A Latin version, still in Rous' hands when Richard died was altered to remove the praise of Richard (see pp. xvi–xvii of the edition above).

P. 181.   These three critics are respectively William Guthrie, 'Impartialis' and Hume.

P. 183.   See below, note to p. 206.

P. 183.   This is the Chronicle by Richard Arnold, (first edition c. 1502, second edition *c.* 1520). Arnold died in 1521.

P. 185.   Milles does not in fact place any particular weight upon these words.

P. 190.   Walpole had carelessly followed Buck in his quotation and not the Croyland Chronicle itself, whose words are *vulgatum est dictos Regis Edwardi pueros quo genere violenti enteritus ignoratur decessisse in fata*, (a rumour arose that King Edward's sons by some unknown violent manner had met their fate). The phrase *vulgus fama valuit*, (commonly reported), comes from Polydore Vergil.

P. 195.   This is a perfectly accurate statement although Walpole seems reluctant to admit it. For this Account see the reference in note to page viii above.

P. 197.   There is no other evidence for such an intention on Richard's part.

P. 198.   Not of course a second coronation, but the installation of Edward of Middleham, Richard's heir, as Prince of Wales in September 1483.

P. 200.   Walpole makes very heavy weather of these two passages, which are not as absurd or devoid of meaning as he would have us believe. The placing of the entry relating to the 'Lord Edward' was in reality fairly arbitrary.

P. 206.   It is probable that this is a slip in the Wardrobe Account for James, so that Walpole was in fact correct.

P. 206.   Thomas Tyrell, Sir James' brother, was probably dead by 1483, although there was a Thomas Tyrell of Heron, cousin to Sir James, active at the time.

P. 209.   Milles infers from the Wardrobe Account that Sir James Tyrell received the office of Master of the Horse just before the installation of Richard's son as Prince of Wales, i.e. at a point in time just before Richard reaches York and when More dates the murder of the Princes.

P. 212.   It was certainly never intended that the 'Lord Edward' should walk in Richard's coronation procession.

P. 215.   Masters concludes that it was not proved that Richard committed the murder, and that any murder might anyway have been ordered by Edward IV.

P. 217.   Masters meant that Lady Catherine Stafford married the grandson of Eleanor Butler's father, i.e. that Catherine Stafford was not the mother of Eleanor Butler. He was quite correct in this, and Walpole wrong.

BIBLIOGRAPHY

Arnold, Richard, *The Customs of London or the Chronicle*, ed. Francis Douce, (London, 1811).

Bacon, Francis, *The History of the Reign of King Henry the Seventh* (London, Folio Society, 1971).

Biographia Britannica, 7 vols., (1747–1766).

Buck, George, *The History of the Life and Reign of King Richard the Third*, ed. A.N. Kincaid, (Gloucester, 1979).

Carte, Thomas, *General History of England to 1654*, 4 vols., (1747–1755).

Commines, Phillipe, *The Memoirs*, translated Andrew Scoble, 2 vols., (London, 1855–1856).

The Crowland Chronicle Continuations 1463–1486, ed. Nicholas Pronay and John Cox, (London, 1986).

Drake, Francis, *Eboracum: history and antiquities of the City of York,* (1736).

Dugdale, William, *The Baronage of England*, 2 vols., (1675–1676).

Fabyan, Robert, *The New Chronicles of England and France*, ed. Henry Ellis, (London, 1811).

Gairdner, James, *History of the Life and Reign of Richard the Third,* (London, 1898).

Gairdner, James, *Memorials of Henry VII* (Rolls Series, 1858).

Grafton, Richard, *Chronicle or History of England*, 2 vols., (London, 1809).

Great Chronicle of London, ed. A.H. Thomas and I.D. Thornley, (London, 1938).

Guthrie, William, *History of England to 1688*, 3 vols., (1744–1751).

Habington, William, *The Historie of Edward the Fourth King of England,* (1640).

Hammond, P.W. and Sutton, Anne F., *Richard III: the Road to Bosworth Field,* (London, 1985).

Hanham, Alison, *Richard III and his Early Historians 1483–1535*, (Oxford, 1975).

Holinshed, Raphael, *Chronicles of England Scotland and Ireland*, 6 vols., (1807–1808).

Horrox, Rosemary and Hammond, P.W., *BL Harleian Manuscript 433*, 4 vols., (Upminster and London, 1976–1983).

Hume, David, *History of England to 1688*, 8 vols. (1789).

Kendall, P.M., *Richard the Third* (London, 1955).

Mancini, Dominic, *The Usurpation of Richard III*, ed. C.A.J. Armstrong (2nd ed., Oxford, 1969).

More, Thomas, *The History of King Richard III*, ed. Richard Sylvester (Yale, 1963).

Parliamentary or Constitutional History of England to the Restoration, 23 vols. (1762–1763).

Peck, Francis, *Desiderata Curiosa* (1735).

Petre, James (ed), *Richard III: Crown and People* (London, 1985).

Rapin de Thoyras, Paul de, *History of England*, translated N. Tindal, 21 vols. (1757–1763).

Rous, John, *Historia Regum Angliae* (Oxford, 1745).

Rous, John, *The Rous Roll* (Gloucester, 1980).

Ross, Charles, *Richard III* (London, 1981).

Rotuli Parliamentorum, 6 vols. (1783).

Rymer, Thomas, *Foedera*, 20 vols. (1704–1732).

Sandford, Francis, *Genealogical History of the Kings of England, 1066 to 1707* (2nd ed., 1707).

Speed, John, *History of Great Britaine* (1611).

Stowe, John, *Annales* (1631).

Sutton, Anne F. and Hammond, P.W., *Coronation of Richard III* (Gloucester, 1983).

Vergil, Polydore, *Three Books of English History*, ed. Henry Ellis (Camden Society, 1844).